Haunted Idaho

Ghosts and Strange Phenomena of the Gem State

Andy Weeks

Illustrations by Marc Radle

STACKPOLE BOOKS

For my son, Brayden
My best buddy

Copyright ©2013 by Stackpole Books

Published by
STACKPOLE BOOKS
5067 Ritter Road
Mechanicsburg, PA 17055
www.stackpolebooks.com

Printed in the United States of America

10 9 8 7 6 5 4 3 2 1

FIRST EDITION

Cover design by Tessa J. Sweigert

Cataloging-in-Publication Data is on file with the Library of Congress.

ISBN 978-0-8117-1176-0

Contents

Introduction 1

Northern Idaho 7
Vacancy at the Bates Motel 8
The Wandering Spirit of Potlatch 10
The Ghosts of Pierce 12
The Railroad Ghost of Colburn 13
The Ghostly Miners of Wallace 14
UFOs at the Top of Idaho 16
Bigfoot in Bonner County 20

Boise and the West 25
A Threatening, Phone-calling Ghost 25
The Ghost Lady of Fort Boise 27
Middle School Hauntings 28
Jailbird Spirits at the Old Pen 29
The Cantankerous Ghost of a Barroom 32
The Intelligent Ghosts of Pete's Tavern 33
The Ghost of Glenns Ferry High School 35
The Haunting of Lake Lowell 35
Boise's Haunted Egyptian Theatre 37
Spooks of Boot Hill Cemetery 38
The Evil Spirits of River Road Bridge 39
The Bloody Walls of a Boise Hotel 40

Wood River Valley 41
A Hemingway Haunt 41
The Spirit of Russian John 43
Bigfoot Encounters 45

The Ghosts of Custer 47
Hunters Encounter UFO 48

Magic Valley 51
Moaning at the Perrine Bridge 51
Playful Phantoms at Pandora's 53
The Pioneer Spirits of Stricker Ranch 55
A Good(ing) Ole Haunt 61
Encounter with a Bigfoot 62
Funeral Home Guest 64
Phantom Voices and a Monkey's Ghost 66
Ghosts of the Ballroom 67
The Drama Queen of Oakley 71
Lady Bluebeard 72
Albion's Haunted Campus 75
Hidden Treasures at the City of Rocks 77

Eastern Idaho 79
The Phantom House of Idaho Falls 79
Emmett's Haunted Bridge 80
The Werewolf Legend of Rose Hill Cemetery 81
Spirits at the Monarch 83
Haunted Hospital 84
No Cheesy Ghost Story Here 85
UFO over INL 86
Ghost Students at Pocatello High School 87
Trains, Lanterns, and Railroad Ghosts 88

Southeast Idaho 91
Monsters in Bear Lake 91
Bigfoot in Franklin County 93
Indian Spirits of Fort Hall and Bear River 94
Ghosts of Malad City 96
Enders Hotel 98

Bibliography 101
Acknowledgments 105
About the Author 107

Introduction

A DOOR OPENED AND FOOTSTEPS PADDED ACROSS THE BEDROOM CARPET. A moment later I heard the clink of hangers being moved. "Heidi," I called from under the sheets, my face buried in a pillow. When my wife didn't answer, I called again. The clinking sounds stopped. She was getting dressed for work, as she does most every morning—or so I assumed. I was still in bed, not having to go to work myself until sometime later. But why didn't she hear me calling? The closet was just a few feet away. I removed the pillow from my face and called again. When she still didn't answer, I turned over, sat up in bed, and looked at the closet. The door was open, but the light was off. Hmm, I wondered. I turned to look at the clock on my nightstand—and goose bumps crawled up my nervous skin. Heidi already had left for work—and had been there for a while, according to the red digital numbers that glared at me from atop my nightstand. So who, or what, had just entered our bedroom, walked across the room, and moved hangers in the closet?

I'm a journalist, I told myself, a person whose profession and lifestyle deals with the facts of life, not its myths and mysteries. But to my chagrin, I admitted that I had experienced enough of the unexplained in my life that I knew sometimes things really do go bump in the night—or, for that matter, during the daytime too.

The sun already was crawling up the eastern sky as I picked myself out of bed, my mind trying to wrap itself around the pieces of the puzzle that had been thrown into my morning routine. Had I just experienced a haunting? Or was it the remnants of a dream being shaken off as I became more conscious? After all, what would a spirit be doing playing with clothes hangers in a walk-in closet?

I got out of bed and checked the closet. Nothing was there except for clothes and the hangers they hung from. After deliberate thought about the episode, I think I may have put a few pieces of the puzzle together. The picture I've created may not be definitive, but it has helped me better grasp what might have happened on that lazy morning in our cozy home in south-central Idaho.

Paranormal researchers have said there are at least six different types of hauntings, the most common of which is of a residual nature. In its usual definition, a residual haunting is the remnant of a traumatic event that occurred at the location—a suicide or violent crime, for instance. The emotional impact of the episode imprints itself on space and time, so to speak, and like a recording, plays itself over and over again. I believe, however, that such a "haunting" need not always be from a traumatic event. Life itself is full of energy, so why wouldn't our actions—however mundane they might seem to us—such as rustling hangers in a closet every morning before work, leave an imprint in the space-time continuum?

And then there's this: Do residual hauntings occur only at locations, or do they happen also in our minds? For instance, I was used to my wife's morning routine, even subconsciously while I slept. Was it my mind that played the haunting, or was it the house? I know one thing: I wasn't dreaming. The sounds woke me, and I lay in bed awake listening to the hangers move.

If nothing else, chalk it up as another weird episode in Idaho, a place of raw beauty and strange phenomena. There definitely is something of the ghostly here, though according to at least one paranormal investigator, the Gem State is not as haunted as some of the longer-settled states in the union. "It's not as active as some places in the East, but that's because Idaho is a newer state," said Jennifer Morin of Paranormal Investigators of Idaho (PII). "It doesn't seem like paranormal investigations are as big in the West as in the East, so there's a lot of undiscovered stuff out here."

The group tries to do at least two investigations a month, and most of the hauntings seem to be of residential homes. "There's a lot of debunking that goes on in residential homes," she said, adding that the genuine ghost activity they do find usually is quite rambunctious. In one home her group was called to investigate, for instance, the homeowners had been attacked and scratched by unseen entities. When the investigators showed up, they told the spirits that they would have to leave the house, because it now belonged to the living people who currently resided there. "Things quieted down after that," said Morin, who's experienced quite a few weird things since she started investigating with her dad.

Morin's first paranormal experience happened when she was just seventeen. She was living with her father in Virginia at the time. Her father's house was nestled in a neighborhood that sat near an old Indian trail, she said, and she often wondered about the trail's history. What were the Indians like who once lived there and used the trail? One night she found out. She got out of bed to use the bathroom and was startled by the apparition of a large Indian standing in the hallway. "It was a full-bodied apparition," Morin said. "I could see the paint on his chest, everything. I turned away for a moment, and when I looked back, he was gone."

Morin, who described the experience in a phone interview on July 10, 2012, said the Indian's spirit was a calming presence. She didn't feel any fear or threat during the encounter. It was her dad's basement that frightened her, a room she would not visit by herself. "Whatever was going on in the basement was the exact opposite [of what I felt with the Indian spirit]. I never went into the basement alone."

There are few explanations for the sighting of an apparition. Was Morin dreaming or sleepwalking when she encountered the alleged Indian spirit? No, she said. She was fully awake. Her bladder told her so, which is why she rose from bed in the first place.

She shared the experience with her dad, and they started talking about life's paranormal mysteries. Because her dad was a Civil War buff who had visited Gettysburg on numerous occasions, often touring its allegedly haunted sites, they decided to start ghost hunting together. When Morin moved to Nampa, Idaho, a year later, she joined PII. Her curiosity for exploring the unknown hasn't left her, and she's had many experiences with the unexplained since that night at her dad's Virginia home.

That's how it is with some people. For some reason they're attuned to the supernatural, while others are numb to such experiences and sensations. What is it that makes certain people receptive to paranormal activity and others ignorant of it?

And what is it about places? Why are some places more haunted than others? Morin says it's about the people. Plain and simple, Idaho doesn't have as many as other states. But I disagree with Morin on one account: There is no dearth of ghost stories here. I found enough to fill this book and had to leave others to float in the recesses of my own mind or computer files.

I hope you'll enjoy reading the ones I've chosen. Some of the stories came from the historical record or are well-known legends, at least in paranormal circles, and others were told to me by real people.

The unusual in the Gem State begins with its name. "Idaho," lobbyist George M. Willing stated in the early 1860s, was a term derived from the Shoshone language, meaning "the sun comes from the mountains" or "gem of the mountains." It was reported that Willing later admitted he had made up the name himself. It was too good a name to forget, apparently, and it stuck. "Idaho County" was established as part of Washington Territory and later was used to create Idaho Territory in 1863. Idaho was admitted to the union on July 3, 1890, becoming the country's forty-third state. Its alleged Shoshone derivative—"gem of the mountains"—wasn't far off base. Idaho has been nicknamed the Gem State, because just about every known gemstone has been found here. More accurately, however, at least to the people who enjoy recreation here, it is a gem because of its open space and mountain wilderness (perhaps one of the benefits of the state not being heavily populated).

There's also plenty of farmland, dairies, and of course potato fields here—and a little bit of folklore associated with the vegetable. Spuds in Idaho are so big, goes one story, that one day a man asked if he could purchase a hundred pounds of potato. "No, sir," the farmer replied. "You either purchase the whole potato or none at all." Another story: One day a farmer's wife had to call on neighbors to help roll a potato off her husband, who had become trapped under it.

The ghost stories contained in this book, however, aren't as funny, although there are some ghosts who try to be comical, such as the little lost ghost girl who plays pranks on a business owner in downtown Twin Falls. On many mornings, Sue McLimans would go to her office to find storage bins opened, the contents scattered about the room. What kind of a haunting is that?

Here's how paranormal researchers, those who've made it their life's ambition to study the mystery, classify the different types of hauntings.

- **Residual.** Often when a traumatic event occurs, the negative energy of the act is "blasted" into the atmosphere and then, like a recording, can play itself over and over again. I believe, however, as I mentioned above, that residual activity need not be from negative energy, but can also be from the positive energy of life itself. Most Idaho hauntings are considered residual in nature, something left over from the past.
- **Intelligent.** Whenever ghost hunters investigate a site, they ask questions in hopes that unseen presences will answer them in some way, whether it's by a disembodied voice, making knocking sounds, or by moving an object. This interactive play is an example of an intelligent haunting, in which the entity is in real time trying to communicate with humans.
- **Poltergeist.** If you see objects move of their own volition, they likely are caused by a poltergeist, believed to be projected by the human mind. Poltergeists have been theorized to be associated with adolescents, especially young women who experience significant stress associated with menstruation or other conditions. Stephen King played up on this theory in his first novel, *Carrie*, which described a young woman with the power of telekinesis, a similar phenomena in which a person has the ability to move objects with the mind.
- **Demons.** Ask any paranormal investigator and they'll tell you the most frightening entities they could encounter are demons, which are malicious spirits that scare, torment, and often manipulate people to commit sinful acts. Demons can appear as black fog or mist, as shadows, or as misleading spirits. Their sole purpose, said Mike Bower, founder of Realms of the Unknown Investigations of Idaho, is to inflict fear and pain. It is said it takes a religious act, such as a cleansing or blessing, to rid a place of these evil spirits.
- **Shadow People.** It still is unclear what exactly shadow people are, but they appear as shapeless, dark masses, often seen only with the peripheral vision. They can move between walls and have

no human features. Clairvoyants consider them nonhuman entities. Christopher Balzano, author of *Ghostly Adventures*, describes them as follows: "Not quite demons, or at least not classified as traditional demons, they might get their strength from the sadness or fear of the living, or from the energy of other spirits. They never want to communicate, only to be there."

• **Doppelganger.** Ever been haunted by a mirror? Basically, a doppleganger is your evil twin, considered to be the harbinger of misfortune or death. These hauntings, while frightening, are extremely rare. It is the one type of haunting not discussed further in this book.

Not everyone agrees that all hauntings fit into a nice little box. John Brian, for instance, a paranormal investigator with the Southeast Idaho Paranormal Organization, which in 2010–2011 hosted the TV show *Mysterious Destinations*, said it is difficult for him to classify hauntings as a certain type. Brian studied anthropology and said ghost hunting for him is another way to study humanity—just another dimension of it. "That's the anthropologist in me," he said, referring to his belief that ghosts try to communicate any way they can. Sometimes it might even be with a physical scratch. Does that mean the spirit is evil? Not necessarily, he said. It might be the only way it knows how to get your attention.

In the following pages you'll read about a number of restless spirits, residual hauntings, shadow people, strange creatures, unidentified flying objects, and other unexplained phenomena that affirm that the Gem State is not only spud country, but also Haunted Idaho.

Northern Idaho

IDAHO'S PANHANDLE IS ONE OF THE MOST SCENIC AREAS IN THE STATE, A true gem. But getting here from the state's lower reaches isn't easy. You either have to travel by highway through eastern Idaho and western Montana, come by way of Washington, or take the much more deliberate route through the state's center and its mountainous passes. Once you reach the panhandle, however, you might not want to leave because of the raw beauty of the place. Look a little closer, though, and you might notice some very unnatural occurrences, such as ghosts, strange creatures, and unidentified flying objects in the sky. If you're a horror movie buff, you might appreciate this chapter's first story, about a creepy motel. Remember Anthony Perkins? He forever destroyed the notion of a peaceful shower for a generation of moviegoers when he played Norman Bates in Alfred Hitchcock's 1960 masterpiece *Psycho*. The movie has the same effect today. You'll be safe taking a shower in Coeur d'Alene's allegedly haunted Bates Motel, but you might see lights turn on and off or witness a flying ashtray. Read on, because there are plenty more stories, all of them allegedly true, that just might send goose pimples up your arms. Welcome to Northern Idaho!

Vacancy at the Bates Motel

Anthony Perkins did to moviegoers in 1960 what Jaws would do to them in 1975: made them afraid of the water—or, in the former's case, made them afraid of taking showers in creepy motel rooms.

Perkins played troubled motel owner Norman Bates in Alfred Hitchcock's *Psycho*. Intended as a psychological thriller, the movie has more popularly been classified as a horror film, and rightly so. Before the movie was released, horror movies featured mostly inhuman monsters as the main villains (think Dracula, Frankenstein, Wolf Man, blobs from outer space). But then Norman Bates came along and changed the way we perceive the genre.

The movie stays with the viewer long after it is over. *Psycho* has the same chilling effect today as it did fifty years ago: renting a motel room, let alone showering in one, just isn't the same after watching this classic movie. In an August 7, 2007, interview with AMC's Harold Goldberg, popular thriller writer John Saul said that *Psycho*, almost five decades after its release, was still one of the most terrifying movies he's ever watched. "I spent most of the time in the lobby," he said.

Norman's motel was, thankfully, only a movie set constructed on the Universal Studios backlot in Los Angeles. There is, however, a real Bates Motel in scenic northern Idaho that is almost as creepy—if not more so—because of the real ghosts rumored to haunt the place.

"This Bates Motel is the real deal," reads a July 8, 2009, *Los Angeles Times* article about the facility, "a lodging at 2018 Sherman Ave. in Coeur d'Alene, Idaho, with 13 rooms and a manager's unit arrayed around a ragged parking lot. It sits along the gritty east end of Coeur d'Alene's main drag. . . . The following warning is posted at the front desk: 'Party policy: No. Don't do it. Don't think about doin' it. And don't ask.'"

No worries, because chances are you wouldn't want to party here anyway. Rumor has it that the motel is haunted by at least a couple of spirits. There are reports of supernatural activity in at least two of the motel's rooms—Nos. 1 and 3. Visitors to these rooms have reported experiencing unnerving feelings, which, in some instances, have been backed by paranormal activity such as

lights flickering, objects falling off tables, and personal items being rearranged.

That's what people claim, anyway, said motel owner Dusty Van, though he readily admits that he has not experienced any such things in the years he's owned the property that first was used a military barracks.

Built during World War II, the facility housed the officers' quarters of the Farragut Naval Training Station. The installation was named after David Farragut, the first admiral of the U.S. Navy and leading naval officer during the Civil War. Today, much of the land is part of Farragut State Park, which sits on the southern tip of Lake Pend Oreille in the Coeur d'Alene Mountains. The officers' quarters became the motel in the 1950s.

In the movie version of the Bates Motel, Room 1 sat directly behind Norman's office where the young attendant spied on his attractive guest—Oh, how that made Mother mad!—and is where the bloody shower murder occurred. But what makes room No. 1 in Idaho's real Bates Motel the scene of ghostly activity? What about room No. 3? What singles out these cabins from the others as places where supernatural activity allegedly occurs? Was the ghostly guest in cabin No. 1, while still a mortal, a fan of Hitchcock's classic movie? We'll probably never know, for we don't even know to whom this spirit belongs.

"I've got to be honest," Van said. "There's nothing that happens here that I know of that could not be attributed to imagination."

There's only one way to find out. Call for details, as there just might be a vacancy for you. Ask for Room 1, if you dare.

The Wandering Spirit of Potlatch

It's a funny name, Potlatch, but the ghost story associated with this town isn't funny at all. It involved the alleged death of an elderly woman many years ago.

Potlatch was founded as a company town and mill site by Potlatch Corporation in 1905, and became one of the largest white pine sawmills in the world. Within just two years, the village had grown to a population of around 1,500 and more than two hundred buildings had been erected within the town proper, including boardinghouses, a church, a school, and a general store. What was interesting for the time, perhaps, was that the town prohibited alcohol and banned prostitution. Its leaders instead encouraged workers to marry by renting houses only to married couples. It wasn't until the 1950s that Potlatch was incorporated. It saw steady success over the next couple decades, but eventually things began to slow.

The mill closed in 1981 and in 1986 the town's commercial district was listed in the National Register of Historic Places. The town has kept its funny name, and is today a bedroom community for the university towns of Moscow, Idaho, and Pullman, Washington. Its population, according to 2010 census records, was 804. That number is slightly higher if you count the area's ghosts.

An old woman went missing several years ago, according to one legend. No one knew what had happened to her, but residents who knew her best were worried that she had become the victim of a fatal accident or a homicidal maniac. Finally, about seven years after her disappearance, a psychic allegedly deduced the location of the woman's body. Police recovered the body where the psychic had predicted, buried beneath the hard crust of the earth just outside of town.

During the years her body had lain beneath the earth the woman's spirit was reportedly seen in town, often near the park or walking the sidewalks. People who claimed to have seen the woman's apparition believed that she may have been trying to find her way home, since she apparently disappeared after aimlessly wandering off.

Was she a victim of Alzheimer's disease? Did she suffer an accident that made her become disoriented? Or did she become a murderer's victim?

As with most legends, there are many unanswered questions to the story. Another one is this: Why couldn't the woman's spirit, once freed from its mortal vessel, find its way either to the woman's earthly home or to her heavenly one? What was it that allegedly kept her spirit on earth, in the historic and funny-named town of Potlatch?

The Ghosts of Pierce

A number of spirits are rumored to haunt several establishments in the small town of Pierce, in Clearwater County in the central-east portion of the state's panhandle. Pierce is a former mining town whose roots began in 1860, the year of the area's gold rush.

The town, which at the time was part of Washington Territory, was named after Elias Davidson Pierce, a prospector and key player in the gold rush. Pierce had immigrated to the United States from Ireland, first settling in South Carolina before moving to Indiana and eventually to California. The gold fever of 1849 drew him to the Golden State, though finding wealth wasn't his only ambition. In 1852, Pierce managed to secure a seat in the California House of Representatives before later heading to Washington Territory to seek further riches.

Once here, Pierce and his friend Wilbur F. Bassett, of Orofino Creek, made the discovery of gold in the area in 1860, initiating the rush. Prospectors swarmed to the area, hoping to glean at least a little of the wealth promised from finding the precious ore. Buildings began to be constructed, including a courthouse in 1862 that today is hailed as Idaho's oldest public building. A year later, Idaho Territory was established, and in 1884 the county seat, which formerly was Pierce, moved north to Murray in the Silver Valley. It moved again to Wallace in 1898. Present-day Clearwater County, named after the nearly seventy-five-mile-long Clearwater River that runs through northern Idaho, was created in 1911. The river has its own history, for in 1805 Merriwether Lewis and William Clark, on their historic Corps of Discovery Expedition, descended the river in dugout canoes.

According to census records, Pierce had a population of 508 people in 2010, while the county itself was home to 8,761 people. As for the ghosts, it's not unheard of to sense a quiet foreboding in the area where the miners' spirits are rumored to still linger. You can tell they are here by the unnerving feelings of being watched or followed. Slight breezes upon the skin, as if some unseen entity just passed by, have been felt by some visitors, while others have reported seeing shadow figures in the area. These are common reports in old mining and ghost towns. Sometimes phantom scents, such as the rancid smells of sweat or tobacco smoke, also have been reported in the area.

The Railroad Ghost of Colburn

The small unincorporated community of Colburn, located in Bonner County in Idaho's panhandle, once was much livelier than it is today; in 1905, the *North Idaho News* described it as a "busy village." It became popular because of the lumber and railroad industries that eventually came to the area—not surprisingly, since northern Idaho is one of the state's most scenic and tree-filled regions. Nearby Sandpoint, for instance, is known as a "tree city" because of its diversity of tree species.

Colburn, located about nine miles north of Sandpoint, was named after Jean Baptiste d'Armour de Courberon—or "Big John Colburn"—who was employed by the Great Northern Railroad. In 1920, businessman Harry E. Brown purchased the town's sawmill and, according to a short history about the area by Bob Gunter on the Sandpoint County website, by 1928 had it in full operation, employing around sixty workers; Colburn itself grew to more than three hundred residents.

Like many towns of the emerging West, Colburn was plagued by disaster and loss. "One disaster after another struck the little town until today there is not much left that indicates where it stood," Gunter writes. The railroad closed in 1935, followed by several fires that destroyed many of the town's buildings including its schoolhouse, which twice was struck by flames.

The memory of Colburn is disheartening, like failed dreams. Among the few buildings that remain, there also reside at least a couple of ghosts (though there are probably more), one of whom just might belong to Old Mr. Colburn himself.

As the legend goes, on certain summer nights the apparition of a man can be seen walking the railroad tracks, and in his hand he holds a lantern high. What is the phantom doing? It's difficult to tell, because he never seems to stay around long enough for anyone to find out. If it's not Colburn's spirit that is walking the tracks, perhaps it is a former railroad guard, checking to make sure things in the old town are well.

The spirit of a woman also has been seen at the town's cemetery. Reports of the wispy figure have circulated since the 1920s, according to local stories. To whom does this spirit belong? Like the railroad ghost, her identity remains a mystery.

The Ghostly Miners of Wallace

It happened all over the West: thriving towns full of prospects and promise suddenly collapsed economically, forcing their people to leave. The houses and businesses and churches and schools that once were occupied by active citizens are left behind to remain empty vessels, historic tributes to a bygone day. The once-thriving towns now are ghost towns, and for many of them the moniker fits like a glove, for some really are occupied by spirits of the dead.

A number of such towns exist in the Gem State; several are in northern Idaho. One of them, the historic town of Wallace, is a little different. Living people still reside here amidst the spirits.

The Silver Valley town was founded by Col. W. R. Wallace, a Wisconsin lumberman who built the first log cabin here in 1884 along the South Fork of the Coeur d'Alene River. It didn't take long before the town became a booming mining community. Prospectors came by the dozens to look for gold, silver, copper, lead, and zinc. By 1887, mining claims dotted the hillsides. But just three years later, in 1890, a violent labor strike broke out and martial law was put into effect. That same year, the town was ravaged by a fire, as it was again in 1910. In 1913, the floods began.

"Flood conditions have grown so bad all over the Coeur d'Alenes following the heavy rains of the past few days that everywhere men are working not only to save their property, but to preserve their lives as well," read a May 30, 1913, news article in the *Weekly Press Times*. "All yesterday the floods showed no sign of abating, and not until late last night, when it grew cold was there any appreciable let up in the size of the overflow. With a continuation of the colder weather through today, it is hoped that any further trouble can be anticipated and prepared for so that there will be little danger to either life or property as has been the case in the last few days. The high water came without any warning whatever, and in nearly every case, no preparations for it had been made. In all parts of the district, old timers say the water is the highest they have ever seen or heard of for this country."

The greatest damage, the paper reported, was to the neighborhoods of Green Hill-Cleveland and Stewart Mills above the city, where two bridges were threatened and a Pacific railroad car, Engine No. 79, was "marooned in the car yards near the Mill." When the mills were reopened the next day, crews retrieved only "limited quantities" of ore.

Things weren't much better in nearby Burke. "The torrent which rushed down Gorge Gulch carried away the ore dumps of the Moonlight and other mines in the gulch," the *Weekly Press Times* reported on May 28, 1913. "All this muck was deposited near the Tiger Hotel which is built across the river. As a result, the water was backed up for a few minutes when it flooded the hotel and began flowing down the main street of Burke. Before long, the whole of the current had made a bed of the street and a stream of water three feet deep and running at the rate of 25 miles per hour rushed through the town. Every house and building on the canyon bottom was flooded and the occupants were forced to take to the hills for protection."

Nothing less than the sheer determination of its residents kept the town's mining operations in force. By World War II about forty mines dotted the valley. Eventually, like other such towns in the American West, Wallace slowly dwindled. Unlike some towns, however, it never quite died.

Instead of being a ghost town, Wallace today is a historic community that is home to around one thousand people. All the downtown buildings are listed in the National Register of Historic Places. It is a pleasant place to visit, if you like history and the outdoors, for here amid the rustic beauty of northern Idaho there is much to learn about the area's colorful past and plenty to do in the way of recreation. There's also ghost story or two here, including one about a spirit who likes to throw rocks at miners' hats.

A number of visitors over the years claimed to have seen figures dressed in period clothing peering at them from windows in the historic buildings, and then quickly vanishing. Other stories have to do with the area's mines, where it is said that strange flashes of light and high-pitched screaming have been reported. As for rocks being thrown at miners' hardhats by unseen hands, that, according to the stories, has happened on more than one occasion.

If you visit the historic town of Wallace today, you won't be disappointed with the history you'll learn. But do keep an eye on those windows, as you just might see an apparition staring back at you. That, of course, would be icing on the cake—to see a period ghost in a town that still very much resembles the past.

UFOs at the Top of Idaho

What lies beyond the starry heavens? It is a question that man has asked ever since he first turned his head upward. The Old Testament prophet Ezekiel saw visions of mysterious creatures and what appeared to be a flying object with "a brightness . . . about it," which has been identified by UFO buffs in our day as a close encounter of another kind. The prophet's eyewitness account, recorded in about 539 B.C., reads in part:

> And I looked, and, behold, a whirlwind came out of the north, a great cloud, and a fire infolding itself, and a brightness was about it, and out of the midst thereof as the colour of amber, out of the midst of the fire.
>
> Also out of the midst thereof came the likeness of four living creatures. And this was their appearance; they had the likeness of a man. . . .
>
> Now as I beheld the living creatures, behold one wheel upon the earth by the living creatures, with his four faces.
>
> The appearance of the wheels and their work was like unto the colour of a beryl: and they four had one likeness: and their appearance and their work was as it were a wheel in the middle of a wheel.
>
> As for their rings, they were so high that they were dreadful; and their rings were full of eyes round about them four.
>
> And when the living creatures went, the wheels went by them: and when the living creatures were lifted up from the earth, the wheels were lifted up.
>
> And under the firmament were their wings straight, the one toward the other: every one had two, which covered on this side, and every one had two, which covered on that side, their bodies.

And when they went, I heard the noise of their wings, like the noise of great waters, as the voice of the Almighty, the voice of speech, as the noise of an host: when they stood, they let down their wings.

(Ezekiel 1:4-5, 15-28.)

While UFO enthusiasts hail the prophet's description as one of the world's greatest accounts of an encounter with extraterrestrial life, religious leaders interpret it simply as a heavenly vision, the strange creature descriptions being symbolic of the glories and endless creations of God.

In another historic UFO case, a Yates Center, Kansas, farmer named Alexander Hamilton claimed in 1897 to have seen a UFO, with humanoids piloting the ship, flying low over his fields. "To my utter astonishment," he said, "I saw an airship descending over my cow lot. It was occupied by six of the strangest beings I ever saw. They were jabbering together, but we could not understand a word they said."

The story was for decades regarded as one of the best documented cases of a UFO sighting. The only problem was that it was a hoax. Hamilton was part of the local "liars club," where members would try to outdo each other with tall tales. It was almost a hundred years before Jerry Clark, in a 1977 article in *FATE* magazine, uncovered the hoax.

That and other tall tales haven't stopped us from searching the night sky. Humans have for centuries lifted our gaze to the starry heavens. Is our search for life beyond the atmosphere symbolic of our quest for something—or someone—greater than ourselves? Are we trying to affirm that we earthlings are not the only beings to exist in the universe?

There is indeed something magical about looking heavenward, even imagining that creatures beyond our solar system have an interest in us. But if indeed they do, what is that interest? What is their purpose in visiting our planet? Why do alien abductions allegedly occur? Are those who visit from the outer limits malevolent beings, as is depicted in H. G. Wells's *War of the Worlds*? Or are they benevolent creatures like the friendly E.T. in Steven Spielberg's cinematic fairytale? And we can't help but wonder: what do aliens look like? Do they look like something out of a sci-fi movie or do they resemble us? Will we ever know? Are there really such things as aliens? Or are they demons in disguise?

Whatever the answers might be, a number of unidentified flying craft have been reported in the deep skies over the Gem State, including several in northern Idaho. Here are a few as reported to the National UFO Reporting Group:

June 6, 2012: At a little after ten p.m. a resident of Coeur d'Alene reported seeing a "very bright star" near the horizon, appearing about "five times larger and brighter than the next brightest star in the sky. It looked like it was moving very slowly to the west and then a flashing light that appeared to be a plane passed a few degrees below it going east." As the plane passed below it, the bright star seemed to suddenly reverse course and, after a few seconds, fade away. The sighting lasted about ten seconds in all, the witness reported. "If I didn't see the movement, which was very minimal, I would think I had just witnessed a star go supernova," the witness said. "Although, I have no idea if that would dim out that quickly."

January 10, 2012: Close to seven-thirty p.m. in Coeur d'Alene, a man was walking his dogs when he witnessed a strange sight in the winter sky: five lights steadily floating in the firmament, which he believed to be satellites. After about an hour of watching their steady passing, he saw a sixth that demonstrated "variable speeds." It slowed, turned, remained stationary for about three minutes, and then split in two, each light flying in a different direction. The man concluded by writing: "I am a firm believer in a multitude of life forms existing in this and other universes and in other dimensions" but "this is the first unexplainable/unidentifiable object I've been privileged to see."

April 9, 2011: An observer in Coeur d'Alene reported seeing an unidentified flying object that "moved great distances in seconds" in the night sky; it then stopped and was stationary for several seconds before again darting across the sky. The object, which seemed to emit no sound, was described as being a straight line of "three white lights with alternating orange and red lights centered just below the white lights . . . probably five miles out [of town] and above the mountains in line of sight looking eastward. I took my eyes off [it] for a second or two and the craft had moved almost out of sight, but also stood stationary, till we decided to go into the house a few seconds later. Strange, not acting like an aircraft as I know of or had observed."

August 24, 2008: "I saw what appeared to be a satellite, but then it stopped moving, then moved in several directions," reported another Coeur d'Alene resident, whose account is similar to the second one mentioned above. The man was with his wife and another couple at scenic Lake Coeur d'Alene when they witnessed the movement of the strange light at around nine p.m. "I was looking up at the stars and noticed what I thought was a satellite. This star light then stopped directly overhead in the vicinity east-southeast of the Big Dipper," the man explained. "It then moved in several directions, always returning to what appeared [to be] the original stopping point." Twice the light grew very dim before returning to its original size. "I am not sure if this was because it was moving farther away or lower below the horizon of the sunlight or earth shadow," the man said. "I was telling my friend what I was seeing and he finally saw light move as well."

July 15, 2008: At a little after ten p.m., a woman was driving to the supermarket when she saw a light "very high" in the sky and "going very fast . . . in a straight line [southward] across Coeur d'Alene, Idaho." The woman didn't hear any noise, but said the object was a "very large bright light." Afterward, the woman called a newspaper, airport, and aviation center, but was told nothing that would help classify what she had seen. "I know what I saw," the woman said. "I know my God made this world, why can't he make many more?"

February 9, 2006: A man and his neighbor witnessed low, south-flying lights over Coeur d'Alene at around six thirty p.m. The man first saw it while driving home from an outing that day. The "very large white blaze," as the man described it, was traveling east to west before it disappeared. But then, another light made an appearance, this time as a "dimmer red glow." The light brightened until it looked like the former light. Once the man was home, he continued to watch the light. He saw his neighbor outside, and called to her. She suggested the light was a plane or helicopter, but the man said it "did not act or move like either. . . . In a matter of seconds of her joining me to watch this light, it began to pick up speed and then disappeared."

July 30, 2004: A witness reported this: "I was walking home at dusk on a summer night, when I looked up to the sky, and saw a ball of light that looked a lot like a star, but was too large to be a star. As soon as I recognized that it was too bright, the light began to move as though it was seemingly startled, then in an instant the light shrunk and disappeared . . . in a curve-ball type motion out into space."

April 24, 2002: Three people saw in the sky over Coeur d'Alene what they at first thought was a helicopter, only to soon find out it was no such thing. The slow-moving object appeared to change into a triangular shape and then back to a spherical one. It seemed to change shape a lot, one witness reported. The witnesses then noticed a sail atop the black craft—which had a "white aura around it" and seemed to wobble as if experiencing mechanical problems. What's more, lights blinked on and off around the craft. "One time a beam of light shot straight out from it across the sky," the report reads. "It made the sound of heavy machinery far off. We all also felt a vibration from it. It is strange but the vibration seemed to be very calming. . . . When it was almost directly overhead it started moving straight up in the sky until it was just a little pinpoint."

August 12, 2001: A slow-moving light was seen over Lake Coeur d'Alene. It got brighter and brighter until, at its brightest, it suddenly disappeared.

Several more reports of UFOs in northern Idaho are listed on the National UFO Reporting Center website, each attesting, like the claims above, that strange crafts, whether they are unknown military or something not of this earth, do haunt the Idaho skies.

Bigfoot in Bonner County

Which is most difficult to believe in: ghosts, UFOs, or strange creatures such as Mothman, the Loch Ness Monster, or Bigfoot? As a young person growing up in sunny Southern California, I didn't find it difficult to believe in any of the above. I was familiar with stories about ghosts, haunted houses, and strange creatures that haunt the backwoods across the country, whether from something

I saw on television or from tall tales that my sister, Cara, would try to scare me with.

The stories about "Mr. Green Thumb" and "Bloody Mary" were, to my young mind, two of the scariest. More than once my teasing sister tried to get me to lock myself in the bathroom, with the lights turned off, and repeat the words "Bloody Mary" ten times. If I did that, Cara told me, the phantom woman would appear with an ax in her hands. Needless to say, Cara has had the last laugh, as I never did take her up on the dare.

My sister wasn't the only one who frightened me. So did a television show I remember watching one afternoon about alleged sightings of the legendary Bigfoot, rumored to haunt the backwoods and countrysides of rural America. The program showed the famous grainy film footage—taken in 1967 in the forests of Northern California—of an alleged Bigfoot walking in the woods, its arms swaying. The program continued to explore the mystery, talking with several alleged witnesses of the creature. Some of the sightings happened during daylight, and the stories about them were just as creepy to my young mind as the ones about the sightings that happened at night.

Bigfoot, I was sure, really existed. So did the Loch Ness Monster, that famous cryptid that supposedly haunts a lake in the Scottish Highlands.

It wasn't until I got older that I began to disbelieve. Perhaps that is the curse of adulthood, the disbelief that things magical and fanciful might truly exist in the world. I began to wonder why no solid proof of the creatures was ever documented. Why were all the captured images of the alleged monsters only grainy images, not crisp photographs? And why, in a world of advancing technology—including satellite imagery—could not these elusive creatures ever be found in quantity?

The world's population has grown since the first sightings of these strange creatures; so have the numbers of visitors to our country's state and national parks and wilderness areas. If there is proof out there, it has escaped my knowledge. But like ghost stories, there is no dearth of reported Bigfoot sightings. Here are a few Bigfoot stories from northern Idaho.

Sometime in the summer of 1975, a northern Idaho family claimed to have seen a young Bigfoot near the Schweitzer Mountain Ski Resort in Bonner County. The family of six described the encounter on the Bigfoot Field Researchers Organization (BFRO) website, which allows witnesses to report sightings to be followed up on by one of the organization's team members. The family described the creature they saw as about the size and appearance of a ten-year-old boy but "with hair all over it."

The creature, which walked on two legs like a human, crossed a logging road in front of the family and then "turned and looked right at us." They then heard what sounded like a howler monkey, which the family thought was the creature's mother calling for it.

The family, for some reason, had numerous encounters with the strange creatures. Two years later, according to the report, the same family witnessed what they assumed to be an adult female Bigfoot in the vicinity of the first sighting. She had yellow hair and stood about five feet tall, heavily built but with short legs. "She had long, beautiful wavy hair," the family reported, "long enough you could not see her ears."

Another incident happened in August 2008, when a rancher heard "loud rock-banging" after he turned off his machinery at the end of a work day. He wondered what he had heard. Maybe it was his ears getting settled to the quiet. But no, the banging started up again, and this time he was able to pinpoint where it was coming from: the thicket of trees not far away.

The man began to inspect the area with one of his Great Pyrenees dogs he had with him that day, and soon realized he was close enough to have "seen the source of the rock banging had it not been hidden by the shadows of the timber," according to the BFRO report. "His normally brave guard dog was alert and focused, but did not attempt to approach the area from which the sound was coming."

An unnerving feeling came upon the man, and he felt as if he were being watched. The eyes were somewhere in the forest. The banging would stop briefly before starting over again. Besides the unnatural noise, he heard no other sounds of nature. The man decided not to investigate further, and instead packed himself and his dog into his pickup truck and left.

A couple weeks later, the man was in the area again when he spotted some large footprints. One print measured twenty-three inches long, while another measured twenty-one inches long.

"Scrape marks were visible at the tip of the toes on the longest print," which were "not claw marks," the man reported, but instead resembled a "long, wide toenail."

The man decided to use modern technology to help him solve the mystery. He placed a game camera in the timber near where he heard the banging noises. The camera, a high-quality model sensitive to movement, was left there for more than a week. The camera never caught any images of Bigfoot or, for that matter, any other creature. "Wind moving trees had triggered it," according to the report, "but not a single animal was photographed."

The man did report seeing a pine tree that had been curiously stripped of its bark about eight to ten feet up the trunk. "Whether it is related to the rock bangs and footprints is unclear at this time," the report reads.

I find these stories interesting, though I have not yet decided whether I believe Bigfoot really exists. I do believe this world is full of mystery and the unexplained, and one of these mysteries is the legend of Bigfoot. It is the same with ghost tales: How do you know if ghosts truly exist, unless you've experienced one for yourself? Maybe that is the way it should be; maybe the unknown remains unknowable to keep the mystery alive.

Boise and the West

BOISE, THE LARGEST CITY IN IDAHO AND THE STATE CAPITAL, IS HOME TO more than two hundred thousand people. It is the largest city between Salt Lake City, Utah, and Portland, Oregon. Most of the metropolitan area lies on a broad, flat plain, with the foothills of the Rocky Mountains rising to the east. Boise is a cozy community that still offers all the urban amenities. But it isn't the only city you'll read about in this section, for here we'll journey along the entire stretch of western Idaho, visiting Mountain Home, Glenns Ferry, and Silver City. Like most other cities in the West, they all have their share of spooks. You'll read about the disturbing spirits of Boise's old penitentiary, high school and middle school hauntings, and a somewhat moody old ghost who haunts a bar. There's more, of course, so read on and get spooked.

A Threatening, Phone-calling Ghost

It is believed in some circles that spirits rely upon the energy of electronics and battery-powered objects in order to manifest themselves. That's the reason batteries in cameras or recorders sometimes die during ghost-hunting investigations. Another common theory is that spirits prefer to manifest as balls of light, or orbs, because doing so takes less energy than appearing as full-bodied apparitions. Spirits are said to have an easier time appearing as apparitions in colder months because there is more static electricity in the atmosphere. These are only theories. But Matt Bower, founder of Realms of the Unknown Investigations of Idaho, believes there might be something to them.

Once, while watching the TV show *Ghost Hunters* in the master bedroom of his and his girlfriend's Meridian home, Bower noticed his cell phone, which was turned off, come alive. "Okay, this is strange," he thought to himself. "Here I am watching *Ghost Hunters* and my phone turns on." He then watched the "record" light come on, and a few seconds later a message told him he had a new voicemail.

He called his girlfriend, who was in the other room, and when she came into the bedroom, she noticed his consternation. "My phone just caught an EVP. It turned itself on and recorded something," Bower told her. She asked if he was going to listen to it. He didn't want to, but decided he'd better. After all, if a spirit went to such lengths to record a message for him, it must be important. So he did, and what he heard frightened him even more than watching his phone record a phantom message: "Get out!" a dark voice told him. "That's the wildest thing that ever happened to me," Bower said. "The energy of that spirit was so strong it actually recorded its own voice."

Did the experience have anything to do with the show he was watching? Bower believes it might have, because he's noticed that the more he's sought out ghosts the more they've found him. "I have to be careful about what I watch," he said, noting that wasn't the only weird experience he's had in the house—or in his life.

Another time, the dark shade of a threatening spirit "grabbed me and held me so I couldn't move," he said. He's had so many encounters throughout his life that he wonders if he's not a conduit for such things. He's been attacked, scratched, and possessed—the spirits just won't leave him alone. They're more active, however, whenever he's actively searching for them. He has since reconsidered whether he wants to continue investigating; he can't sleep at night for fear of being attacked or visited by spirit entities. He sleeps during the day, and at night keeps his home's lights on until the sun comes up.

But there was one time when even that did little to thwart the ghosts who often visit him. He remembers falling asleep with the TV and lights on, only to wake during the night to find them all turned off. Why is it at night when strange, frightening things occur? Bower doesn't have a sure-footed answer for that question. But he guesses it might be because it takes less energy for ghosts to appear in the dark than in the light.

In any case, Bower doesn't just believe in ghosts, but *knows* from personal experience that they really exist—both good, comforting spirits and evil, threatening spirits. And he knows there are demons, which are pure evil and want nothing more than to inflict pain, fear, and unhappiness on their victims. They'll even use a cell phone to do so, if they have to.

The Ghost Lady of Fort Boise

Standing like miniature soldiers amidst tall prairie grass are grave markers honoring the deceased veterans whose bodies are buried at Fort Boise Military Cemetery. And once in a while, a ghost makes its presence known among these markers.

The cemetery was originally located about a half-mile south of its present location, near the Boise Barracks, according to the City of Boise website. But after a flash flood along Cottonwood Creek, 166 graves were relocated in 1906 to their present site. The interments were a mix of enlisted servicemen, family members, and civilians. "A short time later," reads the website, "additional graves were discovered at the original site by soldiers using the old cemetery as a target range. Military activity was halted until these graves were disinterred and moved to the new cemetery location. Additional burials took place—along with disinterments—through the spring of 1913 when the Boise Barracks were closed."

After World War II, the Department of Veterans Affairs decided to close a number of its smaller cemeteries because of funding issues. At the request of the U.S. Army, however, Fort Boise Military Cemetery was left undisturbed, and in 1947 it was deeded to the City of Boise with the understanding that the cemetery would be maintained as a historic site. It was to remain much the way it looked in the early 1900s. Three more bodies, their identities now lost to history, were given solders' burials at the cemetery on Memorial Day 1998. It is believed they were Civil War veterans; their remains were unearthed during flood-control excavation in the vicinity of the original cemetery.

Over the years, insensitive and careless visitors have vandalized parts of the isolated cemetery. "Graves were sometimes used as targets, markers were stolen, fencing and gates painted, and the flagpole was disabled," reports the city's website. "In 1978, the 420-acre parcel surrounding the cemetery was named a reserve by the Park Board of Commissioners in an attempt to retain the ecological, natural state of the area. Subsequently, trails were developed, road access improved, and more people enjoyed the recreation opportunities in the preserve. Increased use greatly reduced vandalism."

It's obvious today that the cemetery has been in good hands, for a number of flowers and other vegetation have been planted in the area, though not all of them have lasted because of the poor soil. Weeds are trimmed, walkways are cleared, and markers have been righted and repaired. The goal of the Boise Parks and Recreation Department, which maintains the graveyard, "is to retain the integrity of the site, respect the land, prevent alienation to the cemetery, and most of all, honor the memory of those who rest there."

But not everybody who was buried here seems to rest. Ironically, I didn't hear any reports about soldiers' spirits haunting the grounds. Instead, ephemeral images of children walking around the graveyard at night have been reported, and some witnesses say they've seen the shade of a woman at the cemetery. The cemetery, located at 750 Mountain Cove Road, sits near an elementary school, and the ghost woman has reportedly been seen there as well. Perhaps in mortal life she worked as one of the school's teachers, but why her spirit doesn't rest can only be guessed at.

Middle School Hauntings

School buildings, especially ones that have been around for a while, often become the talk of the town when it comes to ghost stories. It's no wonder: schoolhouses are places where a high level of emotion is displayed almost daily by students. Could such emotion actually cause a place to be haunted? One theory says that poltergeist activity, for instance, is caused by the high emotions of juveniles during the time of puberty. Could such emotions cause another type of haunting? Perhaps we'll never know why, but we do know that schools are places where some ghosts like to hang out. Emmett Middle School is such a place. Several ghostly tales are associated with the school, the most popular of which is about a music teacher who died while working at the school—but never quite left. His spirit has been seen by students and staff members in different parts of the building. The spirit doesn't stick around for long, though, for after being noticed he quickly vanishes. Lights have been known to flicker on and off in the auditorium.

Another story associated with the building was that a long time ago during a school assembly, a boiler exploded, causing a fire in the gymnasium and trapping students inside. The fire spread quickly and all of the students were killed. It's said if you listen closely, you can sometimes hear phantom cries and banging on the doors in the stale air.

Jailbird Spirits at the Old Pen

Dakota Frandsen visited the Boise State Penitentiary when he was nine years old. During the afternoon tour, he walked by one of the penitentiary's rooms and looked inside. What he saw made him do a double-take: a man was hanging from the ceiling by a noose. "That man is trying to hurt himself," he thought, and then called for help from others nearby. Seconds later, when Dakota turned his head back to the room, the hanged man was gone. The room was empty.

Only one person, Raymond Snowden, was executed in the that room, according to the facility's history. Could Dakota have caught a supernatural glimpse of the deathly scene as it happened long ago?

It was Dakota's first encounter with the unexplained, the sixteen-year-old Twin Falls resident said in early 2012, but not his last. His story is one of many that tell of hauntings at the "Old Pen." The rough-hewn facility is, in fact, deemed by paranormal groups to be one of the most haunted places in Idaho.

A number of groups have conducted investigations inside the facility, among them the crew from the Travel Channel's *Ghost Adventures*, who recorded a number of EVPs and strange,

unexplained images on their cameras there. People claim to have been physically touched or scratched while in the building, and phantom voices or footsteps have frequently been heard; visitors often have felt unnerved or oppressed while in the facility, especially while visiting the solitary-confinement and maximum-security cells.

These experiences are not surprising when you consider the building's history, what it was used for, and the class of people it contained—hardened criminals. It perhaps is only fitting that a place with so much trauma and human emotion would be haunted by its history.

Most paranormal activity at the old penitentiary is believed to be residual in nature, but there have been at least a few instances of intelligent hauntings. While some people claim there are evil spirits that lurk here, at least one investigator, Mike Bower, said they didn't frighten him. But maybe that's because he's experienced very frightening things throughout his life. The activity at the Old Pen, he said, is minor compared to other experiences he's had. Still, the place doesn't sit easy with some visitors, especially considering that the spirit of a very evil man could still be there.

Snowden, the prison's only execution victim, was nicknamed "Idaho's Jack the Ripper" and was executed by hanging on October 18, 1957, for the brutal murder of Cora Dean, of Garden City. On September 23, 1956, he slit the woman's throat, stabbed her thirty times, and severed her spinal cord. The murder weapon was found in a gutter near a cigar store in Boise. When Snowden was arrested, he boasted about killing two other people, though he was convicted for only Dean's murder. He eventually was sentenced to pay the ultimate price for his evil deed. On the day of his hanging, according to the legend, people gathered to watch the incident through a glass window. What they saw wasn't quite what they expected.

The officers pulled the lever, sending Snowden to his death. But it didn't come quickly. The trap doors slammed against the walls, breaking the glass viewing window. And instead of Snowden's neck breaking, he hung suspended in the air, struggling for breath for about fifteen minutes, before finally passing. People sat in the room, watching him twitch and hearing him struggle for breath. It is said that those same struggling sounds can sometimes be heard today when visiting the prison.

The Cantankerous Ghost of a Barroom

The owners of Diamond Lil's Steakhouse and Saloon, Ric and Holly Call, believe the ghost of a deceased friend haunts their Idaho City establishment, and several people claim to have seen the old man's duster-clad spirit sitting at a table as casual as can be, drinking a shot of whiskey. The ghost's name: Christopher Smith.

"He was a friend of ours when he was living," Holly said, noting that Smith now likes to make his presence known by moving glasses and, at times, causing a ruckus in the establishment. He's calmed down a bit over the years, Holly said, but he still is very much felt in the restaurant and bar.

Smith owned his own business, Idaho World Building, not far from the bar, and after work would come in to have an evening drink. He sat at the same table every night. After he passed away, the Calls decided to do some remodeling. That's when Smith let his presence be known. "He wasn't a happy camper," Holly said. "For some reason, he didn't like what we were doing. Things were in disarray."

One night, Ric saw the spirit at the far end of the bar, wearing a hat and long duster. A cook and a female visitor also claimed to have seen the same apparition. Someone suggested to Holly why Smith's spirit might be unhappy: she never offered him a shot, she always removed his ashtray, and there weren't any flowers at his table—the three things Smith liked to have near him in life. So one night Holly decided to leave a shot glass and ashtray and placed a flower at Smith's favorite table. The next morning she found the glass empty, ashes in the tray, and no trace of the flower.

Things have quieted down at the saloon since then, she said, but once in a while something strange still happens that lets them know Smith isn't too far away.

Holly thinks the place is visited by other spirits who, as mortals, once frequented the saloon, which was built in 1867 as a mercantile shop. Over the ensuing years it served as a bar, café, and even once as an infirmary, Holly said. The apparition of a woman dressed in nurse's attire that has been seen in the building is likely a shadow of the infirmary period.

The saloon apparently is not the only haunted building in the vicinity. Perhaps this isn't surprising, considering the history of the area. Like many adventure tales, the rise of Idaho City started with gold.

When the precious ore was found in 1862 in the Boise Basin, it drew the attention of thousands of prospectors, who flooded the area with their ambition and tools. Buildings went up, businesses opened, and Idaho City became one of the largest towns in the territory. The city at one time boasted more than 250 buildings, including bakeries, barbershops, bowling alleys, breweries, drugstores, pool halls, and even opera and theater houses, according to the saloon's website, which recaps the history of the area. "It was a bawdy, lusty town where whiskey was cheaper than water," the website says. "Life was cheap, too. Men went armed at all times and were quick to defend themselves. Winners in disputes often spent time in the stout log jail. Losers were carted off to Pioneer Cemetery."

During the gold rush, more than $250 million worth of gold was taken from the Boise Basin. But eventually, once the mines were exhausted, ore became more difficult to find and prospectors began to leave.

Next came the fires. The first, in 1865, wiped out 80 percent of the buildings in town. Others, in 1867, 1868, and 1871, were similarly destructive. Not all of the buildings were destroyed, however. Some of the town's first buildings, constructed in the 1860s, still stand today as historic landmarks and reminders of a time now long gone.

It is believed the spirits of former residents and mine workers haunt the buildings, as Holly said she often hears a ghost story or two from a neighboring business owner. And when strange, unexplained things happen in her establishment, well, it's almost expected these days. Holly has never felt threatened by the unseen entities, though the ghost of Christopher Smith will let her know if he doesn't like something, she said. But she has a plan: she'll keep an ashtray and shot glass ready, just in case.

The Intelligent Ghosts of Pete's Tavern

Whenever I hear about ghosts at a bar, I can't help but wonder what kind of spirit the person is talking about: the wispy, phantomlike kind, or the kind you drink from a bottle? Is the place really haunted by ghosts, or are the tales just the products of fertile imaginations after drinking a little too much? Grace Stanbery, a bartender at Pete's Tavern in Nampa, claims that the ghostly apparitions seen in the establishment are not caused by too much liquor. They're real phantoms, she said.

"There was one time when we were completely closed, no one else is in the bar, and I heard a female's voice say 'Nine ball,'" Stanbery said. "There've been visual sightings of apparitions—and it's not always due to alcohol."

The Idaho Paranormal Society, formerly Idaho Spirit Seekers, has conducted a number of investigations in the building and just about every time walked away with evidence of the building's paranormal presences, including several recordings of phantom voices.

Stanbery, who's worked at the tavern for about six years, said she hasn't noticed any pattern to the hauntings, but that the entities, whatever they are, seem to be "interactive" or intelligent. "They're not mean, but they let you know they are there," Stanbery said. "If somebody's being a jerk, they might throw a picture off a wall." Stanbery doesn't know who the spirits might belong to.

The tavern has been around for a while and today is owned by Gary Barr. It has a room at the back of the bar that in the days of Prohibition was used as a speakeasy called "The Cave." It is here where most of the EVP recordings have been captured. According to the Idaho Paranormal Society, the group captured four distinguishable and separate voices inside the Cave. One sounds like that of an older male; two are female, one of whom has a Southern accent; and the last one is that of a male "who loves to talk," according to a blog post on the group's website. The entity responds to questions in real time, according the post, "in context with [the investigator's] statements."

Temperature fluctuations also have been noticed in the Cave, and more than one person has reported cool air that, out of the blue, moves past them as if someone walked by, when no one else was around. Others have reported being touched on the head or legs or hearing whispering in their ears or tapping on the wooden bar. One investigator, according to the group's blog, said an EVP recorded a man's voice saying his first and last name before tapping on the bar.

Perhaps the ghost was asking for a drink—a spirit seeking another kind of spirit.

The Ghost of Glenns Ferry High School

There are certain places on this earth that seem to attract spirit entities. Cemeteries, for instance, seem like obvious places for ghosts to hang out. Historic buildings, churches, and schools are others. What is it about certain places that make them magnets for paranormal activity? The short answer, of course, is that a site's history and the people who once lived and died there can influence such activity.

You might not usually think of schools in this context, but the buildings actually are some of the most haunted places. Schools, where for five days a week for at least nine months out of the year high-strung students interact and display all sorts of emotion, seem to frequently be on lists of places where paranormal activity occurs. In some cases, a student or staff member may have died in a school, giving further credence as to why it might be haunted.

Ask your son or daughter sometime if they've experienced anything unexplainable at their school, or inquire of a teacher or principal about alleged ghost stories about the school's buildings. You might be surprised by what you hear.

One Idaho school rumored to be haunted is Glenns Ferry High School. The school graduates about 140 students each year. The students, like most others across the nation and throughout the world, are active in the social scene, be it sports, band, or other activities. Walk down the hallway and it'll seem about like any other school in America—noisy with the din of conversation and laughter. And in the mix, you might hear a scream, perhaps not from a student but from the school's resident ghost.

The high school, according to local lore, is haunted by the spirit of a former staffer who fell down the stairs and died. Her spirit has since been seen in the school's hallways and near the stairs where the fatal accident occurred. Phantom screams, allegedly reenacting the deathly fall, also have been reported in the building.

The Haunting of Lake Lowell

Ghosts apparently are not restricted to haunting only cemeteries, churches, historic sites, houses, and schools. Sometimes they roam the great outdoors, especially if it's where their mortal demise occurred. One such site, according to local lore, is Lake Lowell, about five miles southwest of Nampa, where the spirit of a young girl has been seen on a number of occasions. She apparently was the victim of a waterskiing accident that happened here years ago.

The lake has attracted visitors for a long time. Lake Lowell was created in the early twentieth century in an effort to irrigate local farmland. But the fourteen-and-a-half-mile-long lake did more than provide water for farmers; it also attracted wildlife, including a variety of birds. In February 1909, the Bureau of Reclamation established the 11,000-acre Deer Flat Wildlife Refuge to provide refuge and breeding habitat for migratory birds and other wildlife. The refuge includes the Lake Lowell Unit and the Snake River Islands Unit, the latter of which includes more than one hundred islands along 113 river miles in parts of Idaho and Oregon.

Lake Lowell today is a great place to go boating or drown a worm, which perhaps makes it difficult to believe that anything supernatural occurs here.

Enter the ghost girl, who appears on the lake's shores and rocks—sometimes standing, other times sitting—before slowly vanishing. She looks wet, of course, because the story goes, she was waterskiing when she drowned years ago. Her spirit has haunted the lake ever since.

For some reason, other strange phenomena happen here, too. Phantom voices, which are carried on the wind, often have been heard at the lake, and shadow beings have been seen by more than one witness. Why such entities make their appearance in the rough of nature is anybody's guess. But then again, maybe the answer isn't too difficult to surmise after all. If the serenity and beauty of Mother Nature attracts us humans, perhaps it has the same effect on those unseen beings that surround us.

If you come to Lake Lowell, whether in search of ghosts or of a taste of nature, you can visit only at certain times of the year. The lake is closed to boating from October through mid-April, and the Snake River Islands Unit is closed from February through May.

When you do visit, just be sure to keep an eye out for those rocks, where you might see the ghost girl. Be nice to her, if you do see her, because if the legend is true, her passing wasn't a pleasant one. She could use a smile.

Boise's Haunted Egyptian Theatre

It's been said that some buildings take on a life of their own. If that is true, perhaps no building in Idaho is as lively as the Egyptian Theatre in downtown Boise. You might not find any mummies here, but you could encounter a ghost.

The Egyptian is an impressive, elegant theater with an interesting history. The building was constructed in 1927, during the age of the silent film. In an effort to emulate Egyptian architecture—though Boise was perhaps an odd place for it—the building was modeled after the then newly discovered King Tut's tomb. The theater was called the Egyptian for its unique design, but it didn't keep that name for long. The following decade it was known as the Fox Theatre and in the 1940s as the ADA, before retaking its original name in the 1970s. The building changed looks over the years, along with names, finally returning to its original design in 1999. Today it is one of few theaters in the country remaining from the grand cinema and movie palace era.

The theater, which sits on the corner of Capitol Boulevard and Main Street, is rented for private parties and is used for any number of events, including concerts, opera performances, film festivals, conferences, and even weddings. The structure is one of the city's most-loved buildings, and is known in paranormal circles as one of Boise's most haunted.

"It's not been a bad experience, it's just been an alarming one," the house manager told KTRV FOX 12 in Nampa in a July 2009 report about the building. He was referring to an experience he had while in the theater. He claims to have seen an apparition in the building's projector room and he felt something touch him. "I don't know if there's words to explain it, really," he said. "It's just that you try not to think that there was nothing there that you've actually seen, or that something's actually touched you. Apparently there's something."

The shade in the projector room is something others apparently have seen, for it's been rumored for a while that a male figure haunts the small space. It's believed the ghost belongs to a former projectionist who worked here in the 1930s and possibly died of a heart attack while working one day. Paranormal investigators who've searched the building also have witnessed the apparition and have caught voices on their digital recorders. They say that while the Egyptian is not a threatening place, it definitely has its share of strange phenomena.

Spooks of Boot Hill Cemetery

The story of Idaho City sounds familiar, much like that of many other Western towns in the late nineteenth-century United States. Its settlement was attributed to the discovery of gold in the Boise Basin and the resulting flood of prospectors coming to the area to garner their own riches.

During its heyday, Idaho City had more than 250 buildings, including barbershops, grocery stores, and theaters. For the bawdy, there were other types of entertainment, such as prostitution and gunfights. Many of the gunfight victims, as well as miners, were interred in the city's Pioneer Boot Hill Cemetery.

A series of fires eventually destroyed as much as 80 percent of the original town. It is not known how many victims the flames took. Eventually, the gold dried up and prospectors left—at least, the living ones did. The bodies of the dead ones obviously stayed behind, and so did some of their spirits.

More than one cemetery visitor has claimed to have witnessed the mist-like apparition of a bearded prospector, dressed in period clothing, roaming the fields. In the Chinese segment of the burial ground, it is reported that the spirit of a young Chinese girl has been seen standing by her grave. She doesn't stay long before she fades into oblivion. As with many towns in Idaho at the time, Chinese immigrants helped in the mines.

Because of the ghostly sightings that have occurred here, maybe the old pioneer cemetery should be renamed "Boo Hill Cemetery." But it isn't the only haunt in the Idaho City area. The ghost of a woman has allegedly been seen inside an old grocery store in the city. The spirit likes to walk through the store, looking at merchandise as if she's shopping. When she's finished, instead of moving to the cash register, she heads to the back of the store, where she vanishes through the wall.

The Evil Spirits of River Road Bridge

There's a certain bridge in Caldwell that supposedly is haunted by the spirits of several accident victims. Some of these spirits aren't very nice, said Matthew Bower, who, as a ghost hunter with Realms of the Unknown Investigations, has investigated the bridge many times over the years. Every time he's done so he's walked away with something— an EVP, a video recording, witnessing an apparition, a possession.

"It's not a friendly bridge," Bower said. "It's very haunted. Something keeps drawing me back there."

The possession happened like this: One evening, while investigating the bridge, a fellow investigator noticed that Bower started acting strange, saying odd things. As the crew was getting ready to leave, he walked down the bridge a ways, and then stopped at the railing. His friend watched him, wondering what he was doing. She saw him grasp the railing, then lift one foot upon it. When he started to lift the other foot she ran toward him, pulling him out of his daze before he could jump off the bridge. Bower didn't remember any of it, he said. Those couple of minutes were a complete blank to him. It was one strange experience of many at the bridge.

Silver Bay Bridge, built in the late 1800s, now is known as River Road Bridge. The bridge has been talked about in paranormal circles for years, but perhaps no investigator has had as many experiences there as Bower. He claims to have seen light anomalies, such as red orbs; a number of shadow figures, some which he saw dancing around a friend; and the apparition of a woman dressed in a long dress with two Great Danes at her side.

He also had dreams—which he calls visions—about the bridge. One time he saw himself inside a muscle car, sitting next to an attractive young woman. The girl was talking to him.

"I believe that was her," he said, referring to the girl who was killed at the bridge. He surmised that she must have been in a muscle car when the accident occurred. Legend says that if you cross the bridge at exactly seven p.m., with your headlights off, you'll see the spirit of the woman in the dress on the bridge.

Apparently, Bower said, thrill-seekers used to race to the bridge in their cars, one driver at one end of town, the other driver at the other end of town. Whoever got to the bridge first, and crossed it, won the race. Unfortunately, many of the races ended in tragedy, with the cars colliding head-on, or crashing into the Boise River below, putting an end to both the race and drivers' lives. It also is believed that at least one person hanged herself from the bridge, Bower said.

In one EVP recording, which Bower posted on YouTube, a phantom voice is heard to say "coming."

The Bloody Walls of a Boise Hotel

There's an old hotel in downtown Boise where a gruesome murder took place long ago. The hotel's management won't rent the room today, because, well, the blood is still there—and it won't go away. That, at least, is according to local lore.

When the murder happened, blood was splashed onto the walls, staining them with the evil deed. The blood was scrubbed away, the walls repainted, but the blood kept showing up, as it still does today. Finally, not understanding how to get rid of the blood and frightened by its continued reappearance, management locked the door and now refuses to let anyone inside the room.

In folklore and fiction, hotel rooms have often been the center of paranormal activity. They do make a perfect setting for a ghost story or two, because, if you think about it, in real life they're visited by all kinds of people—persons with emotional problems, sickness, and disease. Who stayed in that room before you? Who slept in that bed? Did anyone die in the room? Did anyone pass away while asleep in the bed? The thoughts are haunting in their own right.

But if you see blood on the walls, that's a sure sign to vacate posthaste.

Wood River Valley

YOU'VE HEARD OF SUN VALLEY, PROBABLY EVEN VISITED IT A TIME OR two. It is Idaho's premier destination, the highest of its highbrow communities. It is a beautiful valley adorned with tall mountains that offer a variety of outdoor recreation in both warm weather and cold. While here, be sure to visit the neighboring communities of Hailey, Ketchum, and Stanley. Among the splendor and serenity of the area, at least a few ghosts roam. One of them might even be the spirit of a famous writer. There's also talk of Bigfoot and miners' spirits.

A Hemingway Haunt

One of the world's most famous writers had ties to Idaho's central region. Death did little to erase Ernest Hemingway's presence in the Gem State. He often is still talked about in reverent tones, and his Ketchum home is preserved by the Nature Conservancy. It is where the writer, distraught because he believed he had lost the ability to craft stories, placed a double-barrel shotgun on his forehead on the morning of July 2, 1961, and pulled the trigger.

Hemingway was in many ways the quintessential American writer. His prose was crisp and simple and his narrative style was all his own. The novels he is best known for include *A Farewell to Arms*, *For Whom the Bell Tolls*, and *The Sun Also Rises*. He cut his writer's teeth as a reporter and war correspondent, and penned numerous short stories, including "Hills Like White Elephants," "The Snows of Kilimanjaro," and my favorite, a chapterless novella called "The Old Man and the Sea," which was made into a memorable film starring Spencer Tracy in 1958. Aspiring writers would do well to become familiar with Hemingway's form and approach to storytelling.

As for the man Hemingway, he was a charismatic and often eccentric fellow who loved the outdoors. Ketchum, with its rough beauty and quick rivers, was the perfect place for the writer to cast his fishing lines or venture into the wilds to hunt waterfowl.

The house was built and furnished in the 1950s by Bob Topping. When Hemingway purchased the house, it was the beginning of the end for the famous writer, who suffered depression once he felt he could no longer write—or perhaps the depression, a vicious circle of ups and downs, caused his writer's block.

The Ketchum house apparently was not Hemingway's favorite home; that honor is claimed by the novelist's home in Key West, Florida. That house, built in 1851 by marine architect Asa Tift, became famous after Hemingway purchased it in 1931. Today the house is open for tours and events, and still contains furniture that Hemingway and his family used in the house. Even the cats that roam the yard are descendants from the ones Hemingway owned. The Key West home is rumored to still have something else of Hemingway: his ghost.

It is believed in some circles that Hemingway also still visits his Ketchum home, though actual stories about it being haunted are scarce. Why? Because the home today is managed by the Nature Conservancy, which has not opened the house to the public. One paranormal investigator, though, said he believed the house was haunted. He had never investigated there, he said, but he had heard rumors. It's difficult to validate the truthfulness of a rumor, however, so the perhaps the biggest mystery is what ghost stories, if any, are associated with the house.

Caretaker Taylor Paslay, however, told *Sun Valley Magazine* in 2010 that there were no ghosts in the house. "There's not a lot of presence in this house," he said.

That's difficult for some people to believe, just as it is difficult for others to believe a place might be haunted.

While the novelist's Key West home was a lively, fun retreat for Hemingway, a place where he lived during the height of his career, his Ketchum home is the one in which he chose to die.

How could a person with such an accomplished life deem his existence no longer useful? It is a tough question to answer. Thankfully, we have Hemingway's wonderful stories still with us to let us know that this man was more than a victim of depression and suicide. He was one of America's greatest storytellers.

Is Hemingway's Ketchum home haunted by his spirit? It very well could be, though the people who know for sure aren't talking about it.

The Spirit of Russian John

Baker Creek, about fifteen miles north of Ketchum in the Sawtooth National Forest, is a primitive campground with few amenities. It's the scenery that draws outdoor buffs to the site, which lies not far from Sun Valley and offers plenty of hiking trails, lakes, and rivers. For starters, there's Mill Lake, practically next door. There's also East Fork Baker Creek, which trout in abundance call their home.

If you visit, be sure to keep an eye out for Russian John. The spirit of the immigrant miner is said to haunt the area in and around Baker Creek Campground. According to lore, he's been here a while, as rumors about the ghost began in the 1920s. It's not known who exactly this ghost belongs to, but Russian John likely immigrated to the United States in the late 1800s or early 1900s. The legend states that Russian John was a miner who worked the area in and around the Wood River Valley. If so, he wasn't alone. Many people of foreign ancestry—Chinese, Germans, Russians—came to Idaho early in the state's history. The immigrants came here for most part to work on the railroad or in the mines.

Today a ranger station is named after Russian John, as is a hot spring located about eight miles north of the Sawtooth National Recreation Area Headquarters, about one thousand yards off U.S. Highway 75. People who claim to have encountered the ghost of Russian John say he doesn't ever stick around for long. He allegedly appears in period miner's garb, with a headlamp on his brow, before quickly and quietly vanishing as if he never existed.

And that's the mystery: Did such a man named Russian John truly exist or is the story urban legend? The ranger station and spring carry the same name, so chances are they were named after a real man; if not, where did the name come from? No one seemed to know for certain. However, visitors to the campground have sometimes found personal items missing or rearranged. Sometimes animals get blamed, but others who know the legend say it probably was just the friendly but teasing spirit of the legendary Russian John playing tricks on them.

Bigfoot Encounters

Bigfoot has become legendary in American culture. Sightings of the alleged beast have been reported by more people than you might realize, beginning in 1810 when David Thompson, a surveyor and trader, spotted large footprints resembling human feet near the Columbia River Gorge. It wasn't until the 1930s, however, that the idea of Bigfoot became widespread in American culture and sightings began to be reported all over the country, from the Florida Everglades to the Pacific Northwest.

Today, you can go to the Bigfoot Field Researchers Organization's website and search by state the many encounters people claim to have had with the unknown creature. Between 1899 and 2011 there were sixty-six reported Bigfoot sightings in Idaho alone.

The earliest recording of a Bigfoot sighting in Idaho was printed in the *Fort Benton River Press* on November 1, 1882. The incident happened in Blaine County.

Two cowboys who had just come in from Camas Prairie related an experience that will probably go a great way toward re-establishing the popular faith in the wildman's tradition. On the first day of this month, two cow boys searching for cattle lost in a storm, passed over some lava craigs, and were startled by suddenly seeing before them the form so often described to them. They were so terrified that they sat up on their horses looking at it in dread.

Mustering courage and drawing their revolvers, they dismounted and gave chase, but the strange being skipped from craig to craig as nimbley as a mountain goat. After an hour's pursuit both young men were so utterly worn out that they both laid down—seeing which the wild man gradually approached them and stopped on the opposite side of the gorge in the lava, from which point he regarded the cow boys intently.

The latter would not shoot, as they considered it would be unjustifiable, though they kept their pistols ready for use, while carefully returning the compliment, thoroughly inspecting the phantom of Snake River.

The wild man was considerably over six feet in height, with great muscular arms which reached to his knees. The muscles stood out in great knots and his chest was broad as that of a bear. Skins were twisted about his feet and ankles, and a wolfs skin about his waist.

All parts of his body to be seen were covered by long black hair, while from his head the hair flowed over his shoulders in coarse, tangled rolls, and mixed with a heavy beard.

His face was dark and swarthy, and his eyes shown brightly, while two tusks protruded from his mouth. His fingers were in the shape of claws, with long, sharp nails, and he acted very much as a wild animal which is unaccustomed to seeing a man.

The boys made all kinds of noises at the sound of which he twisted his head from side to side and moaned—[apparently] he could not give them any "back talk", so, wearying of eyeing him, the two boys fired their revolvers, whereupon the wildman turned a double somersault, and jumped fifteen feet to a low bench and [disappeared], growling terribly as he went.

It is supposed that this is the same apparition that has so often been seen before. The man, no doubt, does as the [I]ndians did for subalstance, and lives on camas root, which grows wild in the area, and he no doubt kills young stock as many yearlings and calves [disappear] mysteriously, and nothing but skeletons are ever found.

The boys at the stock camp are arranging to go out on a scout again to overtake him, being provided with lariats they will lasso him and bring him to Hailey to deliver him up to the county authorities.

The Ghosts of Custer

A ghost town, by its literal definition, means a town that no longer is inhabited by humans. The buildings are but empty vessels, attesting to a day that no longer exists. In the western United States, these sites were typically mining towns, which served prospectors as they hunted for gold and other precious ore. Saloons and brothels were common businesses. It's fun to visit these towns, to see the old buildings, learn about their history, and imagine what life was like all those many years ago.

There are a couple such towns northeast of Stanley, called Custer and Bonanza. Both these towns today are part of Land of the Yankee Fork State Park, operated by the Idaho Department of Parks and Recreation, Challis National Forest, and the Challis District of the Bureau of Land Management. When visiting these towns today, you can see a number of the area's historic buildings, learn from the park's interpretive programs, or, depending on the time of year, watch a reenactment of an Old West shootout. And if you're lucky, you may get to see a ghost or two.

At least one room in one of the buildings in Custer is haunted by the spirit of a young woman in a white dress, said paranormal investigator John Brian. "She's been seen by most people who've worked there and by some of the visitors," he said, noting that the apparition appears in a room in the general store. "We're not sure who she is, but they think it used to be her room."

Three other ghost girls allegedly haunt a trail near a hillside outside Custer. According to the story, the girls, who lived in the area in the late 1800s, were killed when a landslide happened on the mountain, destroying their home. Visitors can walk up to the house today, or what's left of it, anyway. If you decide to take the journey, you might not want to do it at night, for that is when the ghost girls are often seen. They appear very much like they did in real life, holding hands with each other as they make their way up the trail to their earthly abode.

Near the Bonanza portion of the park, it is said the spirit of a woman and her new groom haunt the woods. They're a little upset, because they were both murdered soon after their wedding. The alleged perpetrator was a man who, it was believed by all the townsfolk at the time, wanted to marry the redheaded beauty.

When she turned around and married someone else instead, he became angry and killed both the woman and her groom.

"There was a lot of superstition surrounding the murder," Brian said. "The guy who was her former boyfriend, the guy who was supposed to be her groom, took care of the funerals. But instead of putting the date of the murder on the headstone, he put their wedding date on it instead. And he included the woman's original surname, not her new married name on it." The married couple was buried in a nearby cemetery, but afterward their spirits allegedly were seen in the woods. Some townsfolk wondered if their spirits were cursed. They didn't want to anger the spirits any further, so they never interred anyone else in the cemetery, but instead created a new one behind the town proper.

As for the former boyfriend, he moved to Bozeman, Montana, and sometime later was found dead in his cabin. Clutched in his hands was a handkerchief belonging to his former girlfriend, the woman who he always believed should have married him and not anyone else. Some believe the murdered woman vented her anger by striking back, visiting the man in his Montana cabin and killing him.

Bonanza and Custer: interesting towns, interesting tales.

Hunters Encounter UFO

Blue jeans and rifles are popular items in the Wood River Valley— the blue jeans for any number of reasons, the rifles for one: hunting. Every year hunters from Idaho and neighboring states come to this region to track and harvest game animals, big and small. For many, going afield with a rifle isn't so much about bagging game as it is about enjoying nature and roughing it with family or friends. To a great many folks, just being in the open wilderness, viewing nature at its finest, is reward enough.

There are times, however, when unsuspecting campers or hunters encounter more than they bargained for in the rough, untamed wilderness. While they might view a variety of wildlife, some claim to also have witnessed things they say are unnatural— or at least unearthly.

Four hunters claimed to have encountered a large, triangular flying object that hovered above them for several minutes near their campsite somewhere in the Wood River Valley on September 27, 2000. The story, as told to National UFO Reporting Center (NUFORC) website, goes like this:

While at the campground, one of the hunters left his friends and walked back to his pickup, several yards away, to retrieve some food for his storage chest. He wrestled with the items, still holding his flashlight, and the light pointed upward, shining on a large metallic object overhead. The thing, whatever it was, was huge, as the man later estimated it could have filled a football field.

As fear crept over the man, he fell to his knees and called out to his friends. They saw the object—which they described as triangular and slightly rounded, with white lights at each corner and a red, strobe-like light in its middle—slowly and quietly move toward the nearby mountains. They described the craft's movements as "like a hockey puck gliding over ice—very smooth and unwavering."

The friends, all grown adults, were frightened by the unearthly thing they had encountered, and instead of staying the night at the campground they packed up their belongings and moved to a hotel three hours away, according to NUFORC reports.

The hunters contacted authorities the next morning, as well as the NUFORC offices, giving the group coordinates to their campsite. The group investigated in the area, and found that a triangular-shaped craft had been observed several times in the night skies over Idaho and elsewhere. Some witnesses, with camera or video recorder, had captured images of the unidentified flying object. But even that "evidence" couldn't confirm what the strange craft was or where it came from. Like so many phenomena in the deep and starry sky, the case was filed under "unexplained."

Magic Valley

THOSE WHO VISIT MAGIC VALLEY, WHICH COMPRISES EIGHT COUNTIES IN south-central Idaho, can certainly fall under its spell. It is an open and arid region patchworked with thriving farmland. It also is home to some of the state's most interesting geological features, such as Shoshone Falls, nicknamed the "Niagara of the West"; the Snake River Canyon; Balanced Rock State Park; Thousand Springs Byway; and the Hagerman Fossil Beds National Monument. Among it all are plenty of ghosts, including spirits that haunt an old Oregon Trail homestead, phantoms at a former school campus, and poltergeists at a reception hall. Read on and enjoy the magic.

Moaning at the Perrine Bridge

South-central Idaho has many impressive features, both natural and manmade. Take Shoshone Falls, for instance. This popular outdoor attraction was created about fifteen thousand years ago from the floodwaters of Lake Bonneville. People from near and far come every year to see the impressive waterfalls that cascade more than two hundred feet over rocky cliffs in the Snake River Canyon. The drop is farther than that at Niagara Falls, earning the falls their nickname, the "Niagara of the West."

The falls are a geological marvel of the Snake River Canyon, but they are not the only ones. The canyon itself is an impressive and beautiful rift that winds its way through Twin Falls and neighboring counties. The canyon's namesake river travels four hundred miles from Wyoming's Teton Mountains through southern Idaho as it makes its journey toward a climactic conclusion in Washington, where it meets up with the Columbia River before emptying into the Pacific Ocean.

Back in Idaho, the Snake River and its scenic canyon is a popular place to drown a worm, take a boat ride, paddle a canoe or kayak, birdwatch, or participate in any number of other recreational and leisure activities.

Too bad there's been a lot of death here.

A particularly deadly site is the I. B. Perrine Bridge, an impressive truss-arch bridge that connects Jerome and Twin Falls counties via U.S. Route 93. The four-lane bridge, which stretches about fifteen hundred feet across the canyon from rim to rim, is an engineering marvel and an iconic landmark in Magic Valley. Sadly, the bridge also serves as a memorial for the many persons who've died there, whether by accident, homicide, or suicide.

When I worked at the *Times-News*, it was a frequent occurrence to hear the squawk of the police scanner report a suicide, or attempted suicide, at the bridge. The incidents only were "attempted" if the police reached the victim before he or she made the fatal plunge. If the police didn't reach them in time, it was a successful suicide, for no one who jumps off the bridge survives—unless they wear a parachute.

The bridge is known to BASE jumpers across the country as one of few manmade structures where the extreme sport is allowed all year long. But there've even been some BASE jumpers who've been killed or injured after jumping off the bridge, when their chutes failed to open or became tangled on the rock walls of the canyon.

The misfortune that has occurred here puts a dark mark on the bridge that otherwise is a magnificent addition to the Jerome and Twin Falls communities. People passing through the area often will remember the bridge and deep canyon for years to come.

The bridge, built in the 1970s, replaced the Twin Falls-Jerome Intercounty Bridge, a toll bridge that was built in the 1920s. Tolls were eliminated in the 1940s, however, after the state of Idaho purchased the bridge. Thirty years later, in the 1970s, the bridge began to show its wear and needed replacing. The current bridge was started in 1973 and completed in 1976 at a cost of nearly $10 million. The original cantilever bridge, farther west of the current alignment, was demolished, while the new bridge was given a new name: I. B. Perrine, after Twin Falls's founder and one of the area's most ambitious irrigators at the time.

As for the ghosts, it's rumored in some circles that if you come to the bridge at certain times of the day or night, you can hear the moaning cries of people who used the bridge as the means to end their lives. The wind does whip through the metal trusses, making sounds like moaning. Could it be just the wind that people hear, or is it really the phantom cries of the deceased?

Playful Phantoms at Pandora's

It's been said that cats have nine lives. Buildings in the Magic Valley seem to have just as many, if not more. Several downtown businesses were known by other names during the course of their history, and each time they seemed to take on a new life of their own. That's not to say that something from the past doesn't remain. Pandora's Restaurant and Pub, which now is closed, was such a place.

The building, located in the Warehouse District, was originally used as a warehouse to store grain, clover seed, and beans for the Twin Falls Milling and Elevator Company. It was listed in the National Register of Historic Places in 1995. Most recently, from 2007 to 2010, it was known as a cozy restaurant and bar operated by Kurt and Pandora Handley. The Twin Falls couple said over the course of the three years they leased the building, they experienced several strange encounters with the paranormal.

"The first significant experience we had was in the kitchen," Kurt Handley said. A box of croutons had fallen off the refrigerator onto a table about three feet away. The box landed upside down, and not a crouton had fallen out. When the couple discovered it the next morning, they were intrigued how such a thing could have happened without any croutons flying outside the open box as it fell. Did it fall? It looked more like it was gently placed upside down on the table, deliberately keeping all croutons inside. Kurt said they tried to reenact the episode to see if they could match the scenario, but they couldn't. Every time they tried it, croutons went flying.

The couple also has caught many orbs in the building. Now, according to some ghost hunters, orbs don't necessarily mean the presence of ghosts. Orbs can be dust or moisture on the camera lens or in the air, captured only by a camera's sensitive eye. But one orb the Handleys caught on camera goes against these theories. This particular orb hung over a chair at one of the restaurant's tables. When they zoomed in on the orb, there appeared to be the face of a woman inside it. It appeared as if the spirit was sitting at the table just as comfortably as the restaurant's human customers.

The woman caught on camera might be the victim of an accident, Kurt said. The building has a spiral metal staircase that leads from the first floor to the basement. The stairs originally came from an establishment in Philadelphia. One night, when a paranormal group was investigating Pandora's, one of the investigators stopped at the bottom of the stairs and said that she felt something had happened on those stairs, and that some entity was attached to them. A woman, it is believed, had fallen down those same stairs and died, and her presence lingered at the site of her death.

"A ghost is the disembodied soul of a deceased person who has not yet successfully crossed over," reads a description on True-Ghost-Stories.com. "They become anchored, grounded, or stuck for many reasons. They can and will attach themselves to locations, physical objects, and sometimes people."

Is that what happens when an individual seems to have multiple encounters with the strange and unknown? Has a ghost attached itself to that person? Can only places be haunted, or can people be haunted as well? These are questions that as yet have no definitive answers, though they are subjects that continually are investigated by ghost hunters and those who've it made it their lives' ambition to study the mysterious.

As for what the Handleys believe, "I don't know enough about ghosts to say with any certainty," Kurt said. All he knows is that for some reason, he and his wife—and once in a while a customer— would have experiences with the ghostly while in the former restaurant and bar. Motion alarms often would go off when no one was inside the building, and phantom music was sometimes heard drifting in the air.

Paranormal activity didn't happen every night, "but frequently enough to let us know something was there," Kurt said.

One night he and Pandora were sitting at a table after hours, talking. Pandora saw something to her right, and she turned to see a man standing in the room. "Aren't you going to go greet this guy?" she asked her husband. Kurt turned his head to see who she was referring to, but no one was there. "What guy?" he said. The couple thinks that spirit might have been someone known as Freddy. The gentleman ghost, during his mortal years, is believed to have been an industrial worker; he was killed in the building in an accident long ago.

Interestingly, when Pandora's closed its doors in 2010, Pandora Handley went to work at Elevation 486 near the Snake River Canyon rim in Twin Falls. Kurt said Pandora believed Freddy had attached himself to her and followed her to her new job.

Kurt said they were never frightened in the building they leased for three years, saying it always felt friendly and full of energy. He visited the empty building later, after the restaurant had closed, and said it didn't at all feel the way it used to. It felt lethargic, dead, as if the ghosts, tired of being alone, had found new places to haunt. "I wonder what's been happening at Pandora's new job," Kurt said. "She hasn't said anything in a while. I'll have to ask her."

The Pioneer Spirits of Stricker Ranch

As we sat in the parlor amid period furniture and knickknacks, old portraits looked down upon us from the walls. This was Lucy's parlor, said Gary Guy as he explained to my family and me the history of the century-old house and the six acres it sat upon near rural Kimberly.

Outside on this July day, the sun glided farther west, while inside we all—Gary, myself, my wife and son, and my mother-in-law—had beads of sweat on our faces from the thick, warm air that, despite the front door being open, hung heavy in the room. Upstairs was even worse, but that was where my fifteen-year-old son wanted to go, a camera draped around his neck. He started up the stairs, cautiously, wondering what he might see at the top of the landing, then he stopped near the top. I was still at the bottom, allowing him to show his bravery after hearing the ghost stories.

"Did you hear that?" he asked.

"No, what did you hear?"

"It sounded like a clap, like this," and he clapped his hands together twice. I smiled. "No, I really did," he said. Later, while viewing the rooms upstairs, including one with an old doll sitting in a small rocking chair with its eyes open wide and staring, he claimed to have felt unseen hands brush across his legs.

Gary Guy, caretaker of the property, wasn't surprised. He has his own stories to tell about the site named Stricker Ranch, formerly known as Rock Creek Station and Store.

Life is different at Stricker Ranch today. What used to be 960 acres is now only six. And while the world around it has gotten busier, the ranch has settled down. But bits of the past remain here, such as the wagon ruts, still slightly discernible in the hard crust of the earth, that stretch long and lonely in front of the north-facing house.

On a quiet night—and there are many at this house off the beaten path—you can easily imagine the cowboys and emigrants and freighters approaching the homestead on these trails. You see them first as blurry images, obscured by the heat waves and the dust that is kicked up around them. And then you hear a shot ring out, letting the stage station know company is on its way, and soon the image clears and you can see the worn travelers approach slowly but excitedly. People go to greet them, offering them cool drinks and friendly welcomes.

You can almost hear the sounds, Gary said. Almost.

Gary, an unassuming gentleman, is like that. He can picture in great detail historic episodes of the area, and as you sit and listen to him paint the picture it doesn't take long before you, too, are wrapped in a vision from the past.

Gary said Stricker would still be one of his favorite places even if he didn't live there. It is a remarkable place, full of history.

Rock Creek Station came into being in 1864, when Ben Holladay chose a site on Rock Creek as a home station for his Overland Stage Line, which stretched from Salt Lake City to Walla Walla, Washington. The site became the largest stage station between Fort Hall and Fort Boise. A year later, in 1865, James Bascom built Rock Creek Store. Hundreds of people passed through Rock Creek every

year, stopping at its station and store to buy supplies, relax, or socialize with other travelers.

Even before the station was built, however, the area was a favorite stop for travelers. As early as 1812, Robert Stuart, whom many Magic Valley residents might recognize for the junior high school named after him, described the small river as "Precipice Creek" because "the banks of this stream, at and some distance above its discharge, are almost 300 feet perpendicular."

In 1876, Rock Creek Station drew German-born Herman Stricker, who, along with business partner John Botzet, purchased the house and store. A nearby cellar housed produce and at one time served as a temporary jail. The store remained in use until 1897.

"Rock Creek Store is a great blessing to the emigrants," Sarah Hall Pulliam recorded in her journal on August 31, 1888. "So as they can get a Sack of flour for their selves, and something to feed their starving teams on."

It was at Rock Creek where Herman Stricker met his future bride, Lucy Walgamott, who arrived in the valley in 1879. She came here on the heels of her brother, Charles Walgamott, who had arrived in 1875 to work at the stage station. Herman and Lucy courted for three years before finally marrying in 1882 and moving into a small log cabin on property not far from the store. It was a small home that cozily fit the couple and their growing family—at least until fire destroyed the home, after which they built the larger ranch house that still stands today. The blaze reportedly occurred when no one else was around; according to the legend, Lucy saved her bedroom furniture by hauling it outside one piece at a time.

Lucy took great pride in her home and liked to entertain guests, often throwing parties in her stately ranch house. She had two doors installed in her parlor, Gary told us. One was a door that led outside, the other was a sliding door that separated the parlor from the rest of the house. It was in the parlor where Lucy held her parties, Gary said. When the doors were closed, that was Lucy's time. She was always finicky about her home, but also often opened it up to her friends and fellow emigrants.

It was the spirit of Lucy Stricker whom Gary believes woke him one night to prompt him to ward off late-night hoodlums who had gathered outside the historic site to drink beer. Gary shared his story for my book *Ghosts of Idaho's Magic Valley*: "I felt a hand on my shoulder and I woke up immediately," he said. "I was trying to think what is going on here. I was lying there, listening to the room, and all of a sudden my light comes on. It just popped on. By this time I'm starting to get a little anxious. . . . So I get up and look out the window, and there are about eight people out front. This was about 1:30 in the morning. I really wasn't thinking at the time, otherwise I probably wouldn't have done what I did, but I came out and said 'The site is closed and dark and you really shouldn't be here, and so if you would, I would appreciate it if you'd vacate the premises.' And they started acting like they wanted to give me some flack, but there was one lady there, and I sort of directed my attention to her, and I said, 'I've already called the sheriff's department; they'll probably be here in about ten or fifteen minutes, so I'm asking if you guys would leave.' And she said 'C'mon guys, let's go.' And they jumped in their pickups and took off."

People who've toured the ranch have at times been frightened away by unnerving feelings or even apparitions, Gary said. One time a young woman who was viewing the rooms upstairs ran back down, screaming. She said she had seen the spirit of a young girl in one of the rooms and was frightened by its unexpected appearance. Another time, a man was upstairs but soon came back down, saying he'd rather wait outside because he didn't like what he had experienced upstairs. "I've had enough of that," the man told Gary.

It usually is upstairs where people become spooked, Gary said, and it often involves seeing the apparition of a little girl, whom he believes is named Dolly. Dolly, he said, was an emigrant girl, about eight or nine years old, who became ill and died while at the ranch sometime in the late 1800s. Her body was buried just east of the home, though apparently her spirit has remained inside the house.

Is Dolly the spirit who likes to play tricks on Gary? There've been a few jokes played on him, he said, such as when he poured himself a glass of tea and left the room for a couple minutes to retrieve some papers. When he returned to the kitchen he found his mug half-empty. At other times, after taking a shower, Gary would find the shower curtains moved in a different direction than he had placed them.

Kurt Handley, who would later become the proprietor of Pandora's Restaurant and Pub, worked as the caretaker of the site for about six months in 1997, he said. It was a short stint, perhaps, but it was all he could take. "It wasn't live like Pandora's," he said. "It was oppressive and unwelcome, like the spirits were saying 'this is my house, not yours.'" He said what happened to Guy with the shower curtains was exactly what happened to him on more than one occasion. After a shower he'd close the curtains so they could dry, and later he'd return to the bathroom to find that they had been pulled wide open. Other times, he'd find the furniture in the house moved; not by a great deal, but pushed several feet away from a wall or window, where it previously had sat. Windows would open on their own, lights would turn on and off, and Kurt and others would often see faces in the windows when driving up to the house after being away.

"Are we going to get through this?" Kurt's wife asked him one night after being unnerved by the paranormal activity. All he could think of to say was "Yes, we'll get through it." They did, but they didn't stay much longer. They packed up and headed out, not wanting to spend another night in the old ranch house.

Gary has outstayed the Handleys, but said he sometimes gets spooked by the strange goings-on or noises in the house. But he loves the history of the place and its otherwise quiet beauty. Gary, in a written account, shared some thoughts about the old homestead:

> I've been the caretaker here at Rock Creek for four years now. I've had the good fortune to meet folks from four different continents, about twelve different countries, and about twenty-seven of our fifty states. Every day is an adventure here. If it isn't the visitors to the site and their stories, it's the wild animals that seek refuge here.
>
> The school kids that come out on tours are always fun. They have a hard time understanding how people existed 100 years ago without computers or cell phones. . . . I've met and made friends with hundreds of local families and meet more every week. Some of these folks never knew that Rock Creek Station existed. It is always a treat to meet them and see how often they return to experience the peace and serenity that exists here.

A Good(ing) Ole Haunt

At least three ghosts—but likely more—haunt an old hospital office building in Gooding. The building, most recently used as a bed-and-breakfast called The Get Inn, has as its eternal occupants the spirits of a little girl, a young boy, and an elderly man, according to owners Tony and Elizabeth Woodford. Visitors have seen the spirits, heard them, even physically felt them. Some visitors have been scared by the ghosts. Others have been amused by them. All of the alleged witnesses report the same thing, however: the building is definitely haunted by spirits from the past.

The building was constructed in the early 1900s as one of four office buildings for the Gooding Memorial Hospital. All of the buildings eventually closed and were torn down except this one, a 19,500-square-foot building. The Woodfords purchased it in 2006 and remodeled many of its rooms, for a time turning the facility into a bed-and-breakfast. Many guests have come to take advantage of the cozy setting, and the Woodfords, who also live in the building, said a number of them claimed to have found out during their stay that the building is indeed haunted.

The Woodfords said they've become used to the building's strange sounds, the structure's creaks and groans; such noises are expected in old buildings. Sometimes, however, they hear a door slam in a room where no one is staying or when the facility is otherwise empty. As for more obvious encounters, such as physical touches and apparitions, there are numerous stories.

More than one occupant of Room 220 reported feeling hands upon their head, as if someone were trying to brush their hair. The spirit of a woman has been seen by more than one witness, and one group caught on a digital camera the ghostly image of a boy. Several guests have also claimed to have seen an older, bearded gentleman dressed in a white suit standing at the top of stairs. When a visitor inquired who the man was, Tony said there was no such man staying in the building. A search ensued, but the man could not be found in any of the rooms.

The identities of most of these spirits are not known, but one of them, possibly the woman, could be a family member of one of the doctors who once worked at the old TB hospital. "Supposedly one of the doctors had a daughter or someone in their family hang themself," Tony told me. "There are variations to the story, so how true that is I'm not sure. It could have been in this building, or it could have been in one of the other buildings that no longer exist."

The hospital itself, long since torn down, was built in 1917 as a college operated by the Methodist Episcopal Church. The building sat on 110 acres and functioned as a school until 1938, eventually succumbing to continued low enrollment numbers. Only fifty-six students graduated from the college its first ten years; peak enrollment was 209 students in 1928. After the college closed, the building served in a number of capacities but its most famous role came in 1948 when it opened as one the country's most advanced tuberculosis hospitals, able to serve up to 150 patients at a time. It remained a hospital until 1976.

In the summer of 2012, Tony and his wife closed the adjacent building as an inn and were working toward another venture. But no matter what the building might be used for in the future, the ghosts will likely remain.

Encounter with a Bigfoot

Earth might be a small planet compared to other behemoth orbs in our solar system, but it is huge when it comes to sustaining life. Numerous life forms, many of which humans have yet to discover, dwell in the planet's dense woods, dark tunnels, and deep oceans. The expansive ocean, for instance, is home to abundant sea life that scientists still are discovering in one form or another.

Look at just the most recent two-year period: In 2010, giant craters were discovered at the bottom of the Dead Sea, which, "spewing fresh water and brimming with bacteria," revealed "a fantastic hot spot for life," reads a September 28, 2011, article in *National Geographic News*. That same year, ten potentially new species were discovered during a six-week expedition in the Atlantic Ocean, the magazine reported July 7, 2010. Among the finds was what has since been called "Star of the Deep." The magazine stated, "A rare basket star, seen riding on its intricate network of arms, is among a haul of strange and previously unknown deep-sea creatures." And in January 2012 another *Geographic* article reported,

"Several species of previously unknown marine animals have been discovered thriving in one of the strangest habitats on Earth—next to hydrothermal vents on the ocean floor near Antarctica, in an environment that is too hot, too dark, and too toxic to support most other sea life."

The mystery surrounding some creatures' existence, however, seem destined to never be solved—even though one alleged primate-like creature should, you would think, have been scientifically proven as fact by now. After all, the legend of Bigfoot has been a part of American culture since at least the 1930s. With so many advances in technology, why has no one ever snapped a crisp photo or recorded a zoomed video of the alleged beast? All we have so far when it comes to photos and recordings is grainy footage. And yet, scientists are scouring the ocean floor—and finding new life forms. So why can't we find Bigfoot?

One Magic Valley woman and her grandson claim they found one, briefly, while on an outing one summer day in the South Hills. The creature, said Kimberly resident Carol Sherman, was more than mysterious. It wasn't anything like what you'd see in the movie *Harry and the Hendersons*. The creature, which Carol says she believes was Bigfoot, was the embodiment of "pure evil" and struck fear into her and her grandson's hearts so much that the image has haunted their dreams ever since that fateful day in August 2007.

I recounted Sherman's story in my book *Ghosts of Idaho's Magic Valley*, but it's such an interesting tale that I wanted to briefly explain it here as well.

The sighting, as related to me by Carol and her seventeen-year-old grandson Brandon, occurred on a warm day in August 2007. Carol took Brandon, who was visiting from California, to the South Hills to see the beaver ponds she had found while horseback riding in the area. After taking Rock Creek Road south to Wahlstrom Hollow, just north of Magic Mountain Ski Resort, Carol drove her pickup truck up a steep road and into the forest. Eventually, she had to park her vehicle. The rest of the way to the ponds would be on foot. The two, along with their two dogs, climbed from the pickup and started their trek to the ponds.

That's when they began to hear strange noises—mumblings and a sound like someone banging sticks together—and detected something foul in the air. Besides those odd noises, everything else had quieted. Nature seemed to sleep, which was unusual in such a scenic setting where birds normally chirped.

Suddenly, as they approached the ponds, Carol saw a figure hunched over. When it rose, it did so on two legs, and she could see that the creature, whatever it was, was covered with gray hair. Its eyes were yellow. Carol turned away in fear, while Brandon felt frozen in place. The dogs started barking, unfreezing Brandon from his stupor, and Carol and Brandon started walking back to the pickup. But the creature followed them in the thick of trees, Carol said, as if it wanted to make sure they were leaving. Finally, they lost track of it and drove away, the image of the beast fresh in their minds.

Carol described the creature as "something evil," because of the dread that immediately overcame her when she first saw the beast. Since then, the Bigfoot Field Researchers Organization has investigated Wahlstrom Hollow, but has not come to any conclusive evidence to explain what Carol and Brandon witnessed. The researchers did tell Carol that it was possible that several such creatures were in the area at the time they saw the beast, which would explain the mumblings they had heard. It was like they were trying to communicate with each other, Carol said.

Carol said her "chance encounter" was something that has haunted her dreams often since that summer day; Brandon has been even more affected by the encounter, and doesn't even like to talk about it.

Funeral Home Guest

When Heidi Heil was seventeen, she heard her first phantom voices. It was at a house in Gooding where she lived with her sister and brother-in-law. One night, after she had gone to bed in her basement bedroom, she awoke in the middle of the night to voices coming from upstairs. She thought they must belong to her sister and her brother-in-law, so she lay there unconcerned, trying to go back to sleep. Then she felt a depression next to her in bed. "It was like it, whatever it was, rolled over me, right through me, and got up on the other side of the bed," Heidi said. As it passed through her, "I felt like I had no control over my body. . . . I lay there, scared to death and frozen." The next morning, when she asked about the voices she'd heard in the night, her sister told her they were not up during the night.

The experience left a remarkable imprint on Heidi. It was her first encounter with the paranormal. The second happened a few years later when she was preparing to open her own business, Serenity Funeral Home. While most people outside the funeral biz might find a mortician's job unnerving work, those who do it find it an intriguing and satisfying profession. They want to help the families who are left behind to mourn, they want to honor the deceased with proper preparation and burial, and they often view their work as helping the deceased prepare their bodies for an eventual resurrection.

This basically is what Heidi told the spirits who were making their presence known to her one day in March 2006 while she prepared for the funeral home's opening. While she was in one room painting the walls, a small stereo that sat in a cabinet in another room suddenly started getting louder. "I walked into the other room to see what was happening," Heidi said, "and I saw the volume dial turning. I grabbed it and turned it back down." She said a power surge might cause the volume to rise, but to actually see the knob turn was something else entirely. "It freaked me out."

She decided she needed to confront the spirit right away instead of letting it fester. "So basically I said, 'If there's a spirit here, I want to be friends and work together. I don't want any problems. We have to make a compromise.'"

Since that awkward spring day, things have been quiet at the home, which, in a sense, is surprising to Heil, who not only works there but lives in the funeral home. "Because I work with the deceased you think there'd be more experiences. But I've prepared about two hundred bodies in this house and haven't experienced anything unusual since."

When the renovation and remodeling took place, perhaps the spirits were disturbed by the commotion. "But I just told them that I was living here now. I'm here to take care of people who die."

The spirits seemed to be okay with that.

Phantom Voices and a Monkey's Ghost

Twin Falls, though it is the Magic Valley's largest city, is an unassuming place. It's a place where you don't readily think of ghosts and hauntings, unless, of course, you've experienced such things yourself. Many people here have had personal encounters with ghosts, strange phenomena, and things that go bump in the night.

Eighteen-year-old Danny Seastrom is such a person. Seastrom said he's experienced strange things in his parents' home, which lies near Shoshone Falls in the Snake River Canyon, ever since he was a little boy. Most have been the usual things that go bump in the night, he said, such as strange noises and things falling off counters. Those things can be explained much more easily than things like phantom voices and the dark shade of a monkey that he's both heard and seen in the quiet hours of the night.

"I don't know about the monkey," he said with a chuckle. "I don't think any monkey ever died in my house." But it's the "weirdest of the weird" experiences that he's had, he said. It happened like this:

One night, while playing video games with a friend in the basement, Seastrom heard loud laughter. The laughing, however, wasn't coming from outside the house and it wasn't a human sound. It was in the room itself and sounded very much like a howler monkey's cry.

But his friend, who was only inches away, never heard the sounds; he at first thought Seastrom was joking, but then, as he remembered how Seastrom had told him about the other strange things he experienced in the house, he realized his friend was being serious.

Later that night, when the boys were in their sleeping bags, Seastrom opened his eyes and was startled by what he saw at the back of the couch: the shadowy shape of a monkey peeking over the sofa.

At other times, sometimes while hanging out with friends, Seastrom would hear his mother's voice call to him, or say something like: "Hey, boys, how's it going?" But when he'd answer back, he'd find that his mom never called to him. Sometimes he's heard the voice when she wasn't even home.

"It's always calling my name," he said, like when he'd be upstairs and hear it call, "Hey, Danny, come on down here."

At least one friend, Paul Castronova, claims also to have heard the voice. He said he didn't much believe in ghosts until one day when he was at Seastroms' house and heard the very same thing: Seastrom's mother calling to the boys. But she was in another country at the time, Castronova said. "That freaked me out," he said. "Danny always said his house was haunted."

Seastrom said he's never really felt threatened in the house, just unnerved by the strange things he's seen and heard.

"I think they're mischievous spirits, like a poltergeist," he said, noting that sometimes things would fall off counters when they weren't anywhere near the ledge. "The voices, they like to play tricks on me. But I've not come to any conclusion about what it could be. I have gained a little belief in the paranormal."

Ghosts of the Ballroom

One of the great things about living in Twin Falls is that you don't have to travel far to learn about history. So much of it lies in your own backyard—or, at least in the area's downtown area, which is adorned with many old buildings. The buildings alone have enough history associated with them that separate books could be written about each one. That, however, is not the intent here—though I did glean some individual histories from a number of building owners.

It started with a story about spirits at the Bakehouse, a family-friendly eatery downtown run by Aaron Adams. Though Adams said he did not believe in ghosts, his two servers said they did. Why? Because they claimed to have had experiences with them in the historic building, which was formerly used as a soda shop and ice cream parlor. Spirit presences have been felt in the basement of the facility, said one worker, who noted she one time felt child-like hands grasp her around the neck, as if the owner of the hands wanted a piggyback ride up the stairs. After an old oven that was stored in a room downstairs was moved, it was believed the spirit to whom the stove originally belonged attached itself to the person who moved it. It was not a friendly experience, the woman said. One night after leaving the building, she looked back at the large picture windows and saw the face of an apparition, a woman with a scowl on her face, starring back at her before she slowly faded from view.

I was told to drop by any number of the businesses along Main Avenue and ask the owners what they might have experienced with the strange and paranormal in their buildings. You might be surprised, I was told. Many of them will tell you that they have experienced such things.

I did that very thing, as well as made some phone calls, and was pleasantly surprised to find that, indeed, downtown Twin Falls was a haunted hot spot. One of the places that kept coming up in conversation was a building known as The Historic Ballroom, used today as an event center. But its history stretches back almost a hundred years, long before the current owner, Sarah Taylor, purchased the building in 2010.

The building, located at 205 Shoshone Street North, was built in 1922 as an Elks Lodge, but used by a number of groups and businesses over the ensuing years, including a furniture store, a barbershop, and a printing office. At one time, the Twin Falls Public Library also was located in the building, before it moved to a site near City Park. One of the spirits that at one time allegedly haunted the building was a former barber named Ivan. "He was the longest tenant in the building," Taylor said. "A lot of the gentlemen, manly folk around town, remember him fondly. He was kind of an eccentric character."

Ivan, who leased the building from then-owner Suzy Pferele, used to smoke in the shop. When it came time for his lease to be renewed, Pferele stipulated that he could no longer smoke in the building. That didn't set well with Ivan, who became irritated at the request. He couldn't smoke at home, and now he was asked to not smoke at work?

It was something he needn't have worried about, for before the lease could be renewed Ivan passed away. For a long time afterward, when Pferele went by Ivan's old office, she could smell cigar smoke; not the leftover kind that had stained the walls, but as if Ivan were in his office puffing away at that very moment.

Pferele believed it was Ivan's way of having his revenge, Taylor said, laughing.

She said she's also heard stories about dishes flying off the shelves in the kitchen, though that hasn't happened since she bought the place.

"I don't know that I would attribute that to [the] paranormal," she said. "I'm a skeptic, and so I guess it depends on who you ask. But I know there was so much that was in this building that I wouldn't doubt if there were things that would happen here because it has so much history."

Other stories of haunts in and around the downtown area include:

• Karen Mattice, an employee at Rayborn & Rayborn law offices, tells the story about her boss's dad, E. M. Rayborn, who passed away on January 1, 1986, at the age of eighty-five. Everybody called him Doc, and he was a dedicated businessman who often would come to the office even after he retired. At the time, the offices were located inside the Magic Valley Bank building. Mattice's husband, Mark, encountered Doc in the elevator after he had died.

"My husband was coming up in the elevator," Mattice said. "He had, of course, met Doc while he was alive. Mark said that the elevator doors opened up—and there stood Doc. Doc stepped out of the way for Mark to come out of the elevator and then went in."

Another time, Doc's spirit was seen by one of Mattice's friends while the two were having lunch in the office's breakroom. The friend had never met Doc, but asked who the gentleman in white was. She described Doc perfectly, Mattice said.

• Accountant Ruth Pierce of Stevens Pierce and Associates was talking with a friend via webcam one day when her friend asked her who all those people were behind her. Pierce turned her head and didn't see one person, let alone many, and asked what her friend was talking about. Her friend told her there were several human figures around Pierce, plainly visible through Skype.

It was one of many strange experiences in the building at 320 Main Avenue North in downtown Twin Falls. Pierce said her building is haunted by a number of spirits. Some of them might be the spirits of people who used to work in the facility, which has been many things over the years, including an auto-body repair shop. It is in the second-story loft that Pierce believes most of the spirits hang out. She theorizes that it might be some kind of portal for those who haven't been able to cross over.

• Sue McLimans, owner of Bekins Ford Transfer and Storage Company in the old Warehouse District of Twin Falls, claims she's had many personal encounters with ghosts, including the playful spirit of a pioneer girl that haunts the downtown facility. Many mornings, McLimans would come to work to find storage bin lids removed and the bins' contents strewn about the room.

One of the more direct encounters was when she and an employee were sitting in the main office talking. Suddenly the door opened, and they heard footsteps pad across the room to a second door, which also opened. It was as if someone walked into the room and right back out through the second door.

A psychic friend once told McLimans that the facility was haunted by the spirit of a young girl who died in the 1800s while passing through the area on the Oregon Trail. She fell and hit her head on a rock, the friend told McLimans. "She wears a modest dress with long skirts," she said. The girl's name was Madelyn, McLimans said, but she calls her Maddie.

• Heather Melton believes in ghosts. She's felt their presence and has seen the evidence of their beings. Melton, an employee at a furniture store in downtown Twin Falls, shared with me a few of the experiences she's had since starting work at the elegant but crowded shop along Main Avenue South. The basement is the most unnerving part of the building, she said. That is where broken objects have been found, lights have turned on of their own volition, and oppressive feelings of heaviness often have been felt. She also has seen a shadow figure behind a tall curtain.

• It's rumored that the Orpheum Theater in downtown is haunted by the spirit of a former projectionist who long ago was killed by a fire in the building. When I spoke with employees who worked there, they smirked at the questions about ghosts and hauntings. No, they said. They never have seen anything strange or unexplained in the building. In other circles, though, it has been said the basement of this building is a disturbing place where things sometimes move of their own volition. Ghosts or not, the theater is one of Twin Falls' iconic buildings, reminiscent of a time that no longer exists.

- There's an old house on Borah Avenue West that is allegedly haunted by noisy ghosts, which, according to stories on the *Ghosts of America* site, have frightened the house's still-living occupants. According to one woman who remains anonymous, she'd always feel uneasy in the home and found that items often would go missing. The home also seemed to be a portal for nightmares, because the woman claimed to have had many while living in the house. She never experienced nightmares before living there, and once the family moved away, the nightmares ceased.

One night, her husband woke up, saying he heard footsteps running up to him while he lay in bed. But when he opened his eyes to see who could have come into the bedroom, he saw no one.

The Drama Queen of Oakley

There's at least one spirit that appreciates the arts in Oakley, a small town that sits near the Idaho-Utah border in Cassia County. The spirit, belonging to a woman who once lived in the area, is said to haunt the stage of the Howells Opera House. The apparition has been seen on stage during dress rehearsals, said Harlo Clark, a long-time resident of Oakley. Once while actors were on stage, they noticed an extra "extra" and, once the play was over, asked who the woman was. No one knew, and the woman could not be found afterward.

Clark said he's often felt as if phantom eyes were watching him in the old opera house. He doesn't believe there's anything malevolent here, but it still gives him the creeps whenever he feels those unseen eyes upon him. There also are rumors that the spirit of B. P. Howells, the gentleman for whom the opera house is named, hangs around the century-old building.

The town of Oakley was officially created in 1882 and named after William Oakley, who had opened the Oakley Meadows Pony Express Station, which from 1863 to 1864 delivered mail between Salt Lake City and Boise. By the 1870s, Oakley was becoming a Mormon town. By 1880, an LDS stake was organized in the region.

Oakley continued to grow, and the town eventually opened a newspaper, post office, and city hall. It wasn't until 1907, however, that it got its opera house.

Howells, a magistrate judge in Cassia County, eventually tired of Oakley not having much in the way of culture and decided to build a theater. He began work on the building in 1904, hiring men to retrieve stone and trees, the latter used as flooring, from nearby hills. The building, which cost $22,000, was completed three years later. The opera house continues to put on plays for the community. But according to Clark, it's not just Oakley's human characters that enjoy the acts. Sometimes spirits do, too.

Oakley also is home to the legend of the Hairy Man of Birch Creek Canyon, a Bigfoot-like character that used to chase children and unsuspecting adults near the creature's namesake canyon.

The story, which has become one of Oakley's most popular folktales, has been handed down for generations, Clark said. He remembers hearing about it as a young person and suspects it was created to help keep children in line and prevent them from wandering too far from home. The story is a simple one, without much fanfare or filler: If you walk along Birch Creek Canyon, especially near dusk, you may see a hairy man-like creature come out of hiding. If you're especially unlucky, you might be chased by the creature. Sightings since the old days, however, have been few and far between.

Lady Bluebeard

If you visit Stricker Ranch, south of present-day Kimberly, especially during its Halloween attraction in October, you might learn something about Lady Bluebeard, Idaho's most notorious female. Lady Bluebeard, otherwise known as Lyda Southard, was a serial killer who lived in Twin Falls and is believed to have done away with four husbands, a brother-in-law, and her daughter.

Southard was born Lyda Anna Mae Trueblood on October 16, 1892, in Keyestville, Missouri, but wound up in Twin Falls when her family moved there in 1906. Six years later, on March 17, 1912, she married her first husband, Robert Dooley. Once married, Lyda and Robert lived with Dooley's brother, Ed Dooley, on his ranch. It was there that Lyda bore her first daughter, Lorraine, in 1914. The following year, in August 1915, Ed died from what was deemed ptomaine poisoning. Two months later, Robert fell ill and died of typhoid fever.

Lyda married a second time, this time to William G. McHaffle, in June 1917. Not long after their marriage, Lorraine, only three years old, fell sick and died. The family then moved to Montana, where William died on October 1, 1918. His death, according to the death certificate, was due to influenza and diphtheria.

Lyda didn't waste any time marrying her next husband, Harlen C. Lewis of Billings, Montana, the following March. By that July, he also was dead. Lyda married a fourth time, this time to Pocatello resident Edward F. Meyer. They were married not even a month when he also fell ill and died, supposedly of typhoid fever, on September 7, 1920. It was for Meyer's death that Lyda would ultimately be convicted.

The deaths, though they seemed natural, were suspicious. If the deaths truly were natural, why did Lyda herself not ever fall ill? Four of her husbands had become sick, as well as her daughter.

Enter Earl Dooley, a relative of Lyda's first husband Edward Dooley, who became suspicious about the many deaths. Dooley, a chemist, soon discovered that Ed and Bob Dooley were murdered by arsenic poisoning. Frank Stephan, Twin Falls County prosecutor at the time, exhumed five of the bodies, including those of Lorraine and Bob Dooley. He found traces of arsenic in the bodies. They were believed to be victims of poisoning by how well their bodies had been preserved once interred.

Why did Lyda kill her husbands? These were not crimes of passion or lust, but, as with many crimes, these involved money. According to the Idaho State Life Insurance Company of Boise, all four of Lyda's known husbands had held life insurance policies, and Lyda was listed as the beneficiary. It's estimated that Lyda was able to collect more than $7,000 due to the deaths of her first three husbands.

But what of the little girl, Lorraine? Perhaps Lyda wanted to make it appear she wasn't biased in who she killed. Lyda eventually fled to Hawaii before being extradited to Idaho to face potential murder charges. While in Honolulu, she married a fifth time, this time to petty officer Paul Southard. She was arraigned on June 11, 1921. Following a six-week trial, she was convicted of second-degree murder and sentenced to ten years to life in the Old Idaho State Penitentiary.

"Mrs. Lyda Southard," read a June 11, 1921, *New York Times* article, "pleaded not guilty today when arraigned before Probate Jude Duvall on the charge of murdering Edward F. Meyer, her fourth husband. . . . Mrs. Southard, who was returned from Honolulu, where she was arrested, was accompanied by her father, W. J. Trueblood, and her counsel. She was permitted to leave without guard to consult with her attorneys in their offices. 'Don't let them question me,' said Mrs. Southard before she was taken to a cell. 'I am not well enough to see anyone.' The last 120 miles of the journey from Honolulu was made overland by automobile from Wells, Nev., to avoid crowds. Mrs. Southard is suffering from nervous headaches, with indications of a nervous breakdown, officials say."

Another *New York Times* article, this one from November 7, 1921, reads: "Mrs. Lyda Meyer Southard, convicted here last week of the murder of Edward F. Meyer, her fourth husband, was sentenced today in District Court to from ten years to life imprisonment. The defendant stood up, fixed her eyes on the bench, and received the sentence without a tremor. Notice of appeal was filed by her attorneys, but a stay of execution of sentence was not asked."

Lyda's stay in prison was cut short by her escape on May 4, 1931. She took up residence in Denver, Colorado, as a housekeeper for Harry Whitlock, who she married in March 1932 but who ultimately assisted in her arrest in Topeka, Kansas, on July 31, 1932. She returned to the penitentiary in August 1932. She was released on probation in October 1941, and received a final pardon in 1942.

Lyda—by then known as Anna Shaw and today nicknamed "Lady Bluebeard" because of her infamous legend—died at age sixty-five on February 5, 1958. Her body was laid to rest in the Twin Falls Cemetery, where it is said her spirit does not rest. Stories about apparitions and a strange creature that lurks in the dark of night have been passed about. Bill Knopp, who started Fright Night Tours of Old Town Twin Falls, said there's something unnerving about the cemetery. "I was told to stay away from there at night," he said.

Could the scary thing that haunts there be Southard's restless spirit, who, not finding rest, continues to walk the earth as a tormented soul for the ghastly deeds she committed in the flesh?

Albion's Haunted Campus

If you blink while passing through the small town, you might miss it. It's an exaggeration, of course, but Albion isn't very big at all. According to 2010 census records, Albion was home to just 267 people. It does, however, attract thousands of people from across the Magic Valley every October. Why? So they can, for the price of a ticket, get scared for an hour or two at the Haunted Mansions of Albion, located at the former Albion Normal School campus about thirty minutes south of Burley in Cassia County.

The Normal School opened with twenty-six students on September 11, 1894, a year after the state legislature approved the school, which was one of two in the state. (The other was at Pocatello in eastern Idaho.) The campus was granted accreditation as a four-year college in 1947, the same year it changed its name to Southern Idaho College of Education. During its fifty-seven years of operation, the school produced 6,460 teachers, including Terrell H. Bell, who attended from 1940 to 1942 and later served as United States Secretary of Education from 1981 to 1985 in President Ronald Reagan's administration.

Because of declining enrollment, and over strong objections from the citizens of Albion, the school closed its doors in 1951. From about 1969 to 2006, the buildings were closed to the public and boarded up—looking every bit like a haunted location. Perhaps that's when the ghosts moved in.

Troy and Heather Mortensen purchased the property in 2006, and have since renovated 8,000-square-foot Miller Hall, which was formerly used as the men's dormitory. The couple also renamed the site the Albion Campus Retreat, allowing families to rent the building for reunions and other special gatherings.

Heather Mortensen said she and her husband had heard the stories about the campus being haunted before they purchased the site, but the tales didn't bother them. They figured they'd help with business, since one of their goals was to use the campus for a Halloween attraction. Their accomplishment in making such an attraction perhaps exceeded their goal: it is now the most popular spook alley in the valley, something that fans near and far look forward to every fall. Come October, the lights dim and the paid ghouls come out.

And what of the real ghosts?

They come out too, but not on cue. They usually show up when you least expect them. Though Heather said she herself has never experienced anything unnerving at the property, staff members and others have. Some of the things that have been reported include apparitions, phantom voices, and red, staring eyes.

"We've had a few staff members say they've seen things, and have requested not to work in certain areas of a building," Heather said in a phone interview on April 6, 2012. "If there is a presence here, I think it's a positive one. I think there probably is a presence here . . . because of the exciting and positive things that have happened on this campus. It represented such a wonderful time in their [the students'] lives."

The Mortensens have allowed paranormal groups to investigate the buildings on a number of occasions. One group, the South Eastern Idaho Paranormal Organization (SEIPO), has returned many times and walked away with "unexplainable evidence" just about every time, said SEIPO member Eric Aldridge.

The most frightening experience the group had was one night when the group took a break from investigating and went outside for some fresh air. A pair of red eyes stared at them from behind trees several yards away. The eyes were set about seven feet off the ground, too far up to be those of a man. Could they have been a bear's? No, Aldridge said. "There are no bears in Albion. We thought about what it might be—a bear, a wolf, a coyote. But no way, it had to be something else. There's no way something could have been in the tree. It scared us pretty good. That is the only time I've been scared on an investigation."

In retrospect, what does he think it was? To what kind of creature or entity did the eyes belong? "I don't know," Aldridge said, noting that he still is unsure what his belief is about demonic activity. "All I can say is what we saw."

Others who've visited the old campus have reported seeing apparitions and shadow figures, feeling temperature fluctuations, and having a sense that unseen eyes have kept a watch on them while here. Mortensen said that's from the real spirits that haunt the buildings, and not her staff.

Hidden Treasures at the City of Rocks

If you like to rock climb, you'll love City of Rocks National Reserve. Chances are you've already been there. But what do you know of its history and myths?

City of Rocks, located in Almo near the Idaho-Utah border, is an interesting study in geology. Its granite spires date between 28 million and 2.5 billion years old, the oldest ones coming from the Green Creek Complex, a formation that contains some of the oldest rocks in the western United States. Some of the rocks stand as much as six hundred feet tall.

"Rock formations in the reserve developed through an erosion process called exfoliation, during which thin rock plates and scales sloughed off along joints in the rocks," reads an article on Wikipedia. "The joints, or fractures, resulted from the contraction of the granite as it cooled, from upward expansion of the granite as overlying materials were eroded away, and from regional tectonic stresses."

The rocks have caught the attention of passersby for at least two centuries, and probably longer. In the mid-1800s, emigrants on the California Trail traveled through the area, some of them leaving their initials in axle grease on Register Rock. Some of the initials are still visible today, as are ruts from wagon wheels in some of the rocks. Travelers on the Salt Lake Alternate Trail and freight routes from Kelton, Utah, to Boise also would stop here to rest themselves and their animals. It is believed that the site, though known about by early-nineteenth-century fur trappers, was ignored by settlers until around 1843 when the wagon trains began to travel through the area. Before that, the Shoshone and Bannock tribes hunted bison in the area and would often come here to camp. By 1852, however, it was estimated that more than fifty-two thousand people had passed through the City of Rocks on their way to California's gold fields.

Settlers began to homestead the vicinity in the late 1800s. Though dryland farming declined during the drought years of the 1920s and 1930s, ranching survived. Livestock still graze in the area today. People don't come to the rocks to see the cattle, however, but to rock climb, hike, or picnic. Climbers often refer to it simply as "The City."

While here, visitors often stop by nearby Castle Rock State Park, which also is a fun place to visit. The parks are open all year, but that doesn't mean all of the roads are open; due to weather, some roads might be closed in winter.

One legend associated with the park, said superintendent Wallace Keck, is about stagecoaches that were periodically attacked by robbers. The loot, sometimes gold or other precious items, was buried by the robbers for safekeeping. It is said the loot still is buried here, though Keck said that likely is an old wives' tale. No buried treasure ever was uncovered here, to his knowledge. Or maybe the spirits of those robbers are doing a fine job of preventing anyone else from finding it.

Keck said he's not as interested in legends about the park as he is in its factual history. "We've been doing a lot of studying of the signatures [at Register Rock, where the emigrants penned their names in axle grease] along the California Trail," he said. "We've found that the facts are every bit as exciting as the myths."

Eastern Idaho

EASTERN IDAHO CONTAINS A LITTLE BIT OF EVERYTHING—GROWING cities, fertile agricultural lands, outdoor recreation destinations, and a rich history of Native American lore and pioneer tales. The spirits who walk here are all about the past. There's a ghostly house, in the most literal sense of the word—like a phantom, it appears and disappears at will. That's one of many strange stories from this region; others include a ghostly bridge, a haunted hotel, and a spooky hospital. There's even a story about a werewolf that presumably roams a lonely cemetery.

The Phantom House of Idaho Falls

The majority of ghost stories tell of disembodied spirits that haunt the places they frequented in life—houses, apartments, or other buildings. The ghosts often haunt the places where they passed from this life into the spirit realm, or places to which they held other emotional ties, such as a former job site.

Stories about haunted buildings are many. But one story of a spooky old house in Idaho Falls breaks the mold. Instead of a building haunted by a spirit or residual echo of things that happened there, in this case it is the house itself that does the haunting.

The legend goes as follows: There is an empty abandoned lot in Idaho Falls that is a portal to the Other Side, for the house that once stood there sometimes appears out of nowhere to wary passersby. According to the story, once long ago when the house was still standing, the head of the household murdered his family, staining the property with the evil of his vicious act.

Walking by the lot today, you'll likely see overgrown weeds and trees, and, depending on your sensitivity to the spiritual world, perhaps the apparition of the murder house. The ghost house has reportedly been seen by a number of people, who say its windows were lit up, as if people were still living in the house, going about their nightly routines. Human figures have been seen walking past the lighted windows or at the front door. On a few occasions, the house itself was not seen but the lot's trees appeared illuminated as if lights from the phantom house were shining on them.

Some who've visited the property, perhaps on a dare, have been scared away by sudden screams that emanate from the lot. Those who've heard the cries believe they are the residual hauntings of the former house's murder victims. Two brothers visited the property one night, according to one Internet story, only to be scared away by the deathly shrieks. As they scrambled up the fence to leave, one of the brothers was scratched by unseen hands. At other times, phantom voices and the laughter of children have been heard on the lot, as if the ghostly kids were busy playing in the yard just as they did during their short mortal sojourn upon the earth.

The phantom noises, as well as the shade of the house itself, never stay for long before they return to the netherworlds where they apparently reside today.

Emmett's Haunted Bridge

There's an old bridge in Emmett that is haunted by the sounds of criminal activity, according to reports on several paranormal websites about Idaho. One claim is that you can sometimes hear the sounds of something large being dumped over the side of the bridge and into the water.

Not everyone who visits the bridge hears the sounds, nor are the sounds constant. They apparently occur randomly, to selected people whose ears are attuned to the supernatural. Those who claim to have heard the sounds believe they are the residual reenactment of the body of a murder victim being dumped into the river.

Besides the phantom splash, others allegedly have heard the phantom sounds of children crying at the bridge, and the voice of a mother trying to hush the children. What does that mean? Is this another take on the "crybaby bridge" tale, a legend that many states have?

According to lore, crybaby bridges are places where deranged or possessed mothers drove their cars off the road, taking their children with them to a turbulent end. Long afterward, their voices can be heard calling out to their children, who in turn often are heard crying as their spirits relive the horrific episode.

The Werewolf Legend of Rose Hill Cemetery

It's one thing to believe in ghosts, but how about zombies, vampires, and werewolves? You might be inclined to believe in these creatures of the night if you visited Rose Hill Cemetery, which, according to local legend, is the burial spot of a ferocious werewolf.

According to the story, early in Idaho Falls history a number of gruesome murders occurred that had all the signs of attacks by a wild animal. But most animals attack humans only when they feel threatened or are hungry. None of the victims were foolish enough to threaten a dangerous creature, and there was plenty of easier game in the area for a hungry animal, so some residents began to wonder if the killings were caused by something more sinister. Were they the work of man, or beast? At least a few believed that they were from both—that the killer was a werewolf.

On the night of the next full moon, the townsfolk raised a search party, found the sinister creature, and shot and killed it. They then cut the creature in half and buried the body parts in two separate graves at Rose Hill Cemetery. They figured that burying the creature in such a manner would prevent any supernatural activity from unearthing the devilish beast. It couldn't come back to life if it were split in two and buried six feet under the earth in two different

spots, could it? They then placed a headstone on each burial spot. One read "Were," the other "Wolf."

But as the legend goes, the residents' efforts were in vain, for not even the separation of two graves could keep the werewolf from resurrecting. Not long after the burial, they found the graves dug up and a large bite taken out of the headstone that read "Wolf."

Though this is a fun story, it has all the hallmarks of an urban legend. No further sightings of the werewolf have been reported and, luckily, there've been no more gruesome murders in the vicinity attributed to the beast.

However, there's another strange story associated with Rose Hill Cemetery. This one concerns a mausoleum that has a friendly ghost attached to it. The ghost, to whomever it belongs, likes you to come by and say "Hi." If you do, it'll answer your greeting with one of its own: knocking on the cement walls.

The next time you visit Rose Hill, why not give it a try? Just be sure to keep your eyes peeled for a toothy werewolf.

Spirits at the Monarch

One of the first hotels in Pocatello is also one of the city's most haunted. "It has an interesting history because it was originally used as a hotel and brothel," John Brian said about the Monarch Hotel at 240 West Center. "The basement was a speakeasy and opium den for the Chinese, adding to its seedy past." The building now is used as a low-income apartment complex. The tenants have their own rooms but share a community bathroom. Over the years, at least a couple deaths have occurred in the building, and the site has long been talked about in paranormal circles as a good place to catch strange phenomena.

Brian and his group, Southeast Idaho Paranormal Organization, have conducted investigations in the building and have seen shadow figures, been scratched, and caught voice recordings of what seems to be words spoken from the spirit realm.

"The atmosphere is very different here," Brian said, noting that not long after his group arrived one night for an investigation his wife felt a burning sensation on the bottom of one arm. When she looked, she found several small scratches, like fingernail marks, running down her arm. A little later, while she and a friend went to investigate on the second floor, an unseen entity threw a metal object at them. Brian described the object as something resembling an old needle-threader or button. "After that my brother, who was up around a closet, got a burning sensation on his back," Brian said, though they didn't investigate it until later, when things began to settle down, according to the group's K2 meter. When they did look at the man's back they saw the word STOP scratched onto the skin. "We could see fresh droplets of blood coming out of it," Brian said.

In Brian's opinion, phantom scratches do not necessarily come from an evil entity; sometimes scratching might be the only way a spirit knows how to communicate with the living.

"We take a real different approach to those things," he said. "Most people who've experienced something like this—it's not uncommon to get scratched while ghost hunting—will say that a bad or evil spirit did it to them. In our group, we don't subscribe to that, saying that a spirit it evil. We just call it a phenomenon."

Haunted Hospital

If any place has a right to be haunted, it is a hospital. It doesn't take much imagination to know why. Between the building's complacent, sterile-looking walls, patients old and young suffer trauma and pain and, in some instances, death. For some the pain is strictly physical, while others might suffer in both body and mind. Some patients find relief only when the heart monitor flatlines—but then it's the grieving family members who suffer. With so much pain, suffering, and death within their walls, it is no wonder that hospitals are places where spirits might remain.

Though you could probably find any number of potentially haunted hospitals, the one we focus on now is the former Harms Memorial Hospital, now Power County Hospital, in American Falls. Located at 510 Roosevelt Street, the hospital was named after Dr. Frank Harms, who was born in 1914 in Cordell, Oklahoma, and moved to eastern Idaho in 1953. He began his medical career as a family practitioner in 1940, after receiving medical training at Bethel College in North Newton, Kansas, and the University of Oklahoma. Harms, who was an active community member, was forced to retire in 1980 after suffering a mild heart attack. Soon after his retirement, the hospital was renamed Power County. Harms died of a heart attack on March 28, 1981, while visiting friends in Colorado Springs. Could it be that his spirit haunts the place that was named after him? It might—but many think it's not the only one.

With so much history, it's no wonder the hospital has a ghost story or two. According to the stories, Harms's spirit occasionally visits the hospital, leaving behind the scent of cigar smoke. Buzzers in different rooms also have been known to go off when no one was around to push them. Sometimes, shadow people or full-bodied apparitions have been reported in the corridors and hallways and rooms, often noticed in the witnesses' peripheral vision. When the witness turns to look at the figure, it quickly vanishes as if no one was there.

No Cheesy Ghost Story Here

In 1924, Kraft Food Company opened a factory in Pocatello, where it processed cheese and other types of dairy product for three decades. In 1955, Kraft began to scale back production at the site. Over the next ten years, the company built a new plant to the north of the city, and the old Kraft Road factory was abandoned.

Abandoned, that is, except for the ghosts rumored to haunt the facility.

Over the years since its abandonment, many stories have sprung up about the place. Perhaps the most popular story is this one: In 1984, a man at a party drugged a young girl, took her to the building, strapped her to a chair, and raped her in the middle of the warehouse before killing her. Ten years later on the anniversary of the girl's death, at 3:59 a.m., the time the girl had been killed, fifteen different calls were made to 911 from the warehouse. Operators reported hearing a girl scream and cry: "Please help me!" When police arrived, they found a chair in the middle of the warehouse and an empty shell casing. The casing, so the story goes, may have been that of the bullet that killed the girl, which was initially never found in the initial investigation.

"That place definitely is haunted," said paranormal investigator Mike Bower. Others tend to disagree.

"Pocatello Police and the Bannock County Sheriff's Office both say the story is bogus," the *Standard-Journal* reported. "Bannock County Sheriff Lorin Nielsen said there have been reports of satanic rituals performed at the site or just general vandalism and trespassing, but that's it."

Some people, like Bower, believe satanic rituals are enough to draw creepy paranormal activity like the example mentioned above. But according to the *Journal* story, the warehouse's owner has tried hard to dispel the belief that his facility is haunted. So far, police seem to back him up. There are no ghosts at the former Kraft warehouse, they say.

Or are there? Don't try to find out. The warehouse is privately owned, and trespassing is not allowed.

UFO over INL

The Idaho National Laboratory (INL), in operation since 1949, is a science-based, applied engineering laboratory. The more than four thousand people employed by the laboratory work on nuclear and energy research and national defense projects.

Even more interesting, perhaps, than the scientific projects going on inside the facility, located near Idaho Falls, are the UFOs rumored to haunt the skies above it.

One of the more popular UFO stories occurred in mid-July 2010, during a wildfire near the site. In the midst of heavy smoke, a shiny disc-like object appeared in the skies. Bystanders stood by and watched the object, whatever it was, fly in and out of the smoke. The object was caught on film, twice, by KPVI News 6. Some viewers claimed after watching the video it might have been a bird or helicopter. But it didn't act like a helicopter, others said. And why would a bird be flying around in the thick smoke? Animals generally flee from fire and smoke, not run or fly to it.

The discussion the video drew was, if anything, entertaining to read.

One person, writing on the *Above Top Secret* website, noted: "I know you probably won't be happy with me saying it's a bird. But . . . I've now watched that video at least ten times . . . I can even see the wings extending down and flapping on a couple of occasions. If you look at it carefully, you'll be able to see that too."

A post from another person, reads: "But then again, why would a bird be flying around in smoke? So many questions, so few experts."

One blog writer even went so far as to say this: "Animals are generally smart enough to not hang around in toxic fumes. Do you think it could have been an alien that shape-shifted into a bird?"

And, of the numerous posts on the blog, I share one more:

I accept there are skeptics and fence sitters and this is okay when dealing with this subject. But, you should be able to also accept the fact that there are millions of [people's experiences] with Alien's and AFO's [alien flying objects] and they know what they know just like the skeptics and fence sitters feel they know what they know.

I KNOW there are Beings which we call Alien's [that] exist and they do travel via AFO's . . . Now I don't know if these videos and still pictures are Alien or a bird as suggested. I believe we need a true professional that deals with this to investigate and give his/her knowledge on this, that's all . . . plain and simple. Maybe we will all be proven wrong and it is a pink elephant.

No expert, if there is such a thing when it comes to UFOs, has ever stepped forward to confirm the identity of the flying object, and so the rumors and arguments among UFO circles continue. The rumors likely won't be dispelled any time soon: The video has since been removed from the news station's website.

Ghost Students at Pocatello High School

School buildings—places where friendships are molded and emotions run high—are frequently listed among the haunted hot spots in cities and towns. Pocatello's high school is no exception.

According to John Brian, director of the Southeast Idaho Paranormal Organization, the school has several stories of hauntings and other strange incidents. While some of the stories might be nothing more than urban legend, he said, others are probably very real.

His group has, in fact, documented strange phenomena in the building; they've captured phantom voices on digital recorders and made video recordings of apparitions. One day, reporters from the

Idaho State Journal visited the building during a ghost hunt, Brian said, and they also captured some strange things. Stories abound, according to Brian.

"I know of at least three deaths that reportedly happened in the building," Brian said. One of the stories involved two female students who, allegedly poisoned at home one morning, came to school where they later died. Another story says that a former librarian hanged herself in the school's library. And a young boy supposedly drowned in the school's first swimming pool. A rape also allegedly occurred in the basement beneath the gymnasium, Brian said.

It's difficult to tell if any of these stories, or which ones, might be real or make-believe. Some of them, like the librarian's hanging or the boy's drowning, sound similar to other stories told about school hauntings. But Brian said he's spoken directly to janitors who claim they saw the drowned boy's spirit, dripping wet, in the old school building.

"There's a lot of different areas of the school that are haunted," Brian said. Supernatural entities haunt the auditorium, basement, girls' locker room, gymnasium, and library. "There's something under the stage," he said, noting that his group has digitally captured strange balls of light, phantom voices, and even apparitions. With so many presences, its more than likely the school's history holds other stories that are now lost to the past.

Trains, Lanterns, and Railroad Ghosts

What child doesn't like to hear the whistle of a train, or count its cars as they pass by, or listen to the quick clickety-clack, clickety-clack of its wheels on the tracks? What used to be a common thing for children to experience in America is now uncommon in many parts of the country. Though trains still serve an important function, they aren't as prevalent as they used to be. In some ways, that's a shame, for they are a bit of American culture that is becoming lost to modernity. One day, trains might only be found in history books and museums.

But the ghosts of some railroad workers don't know that times have changed, that the days of the steam locomotive have long since passed. Take, for instance, the ghostly apparition that makes himself known every once in a while at Union Station in Pocatello. Built in 1915 by the Oregon Short Line, the station later was taken over by Union Pacific and is now used as that railroad's offices.

More than one witness has reported seeing strange lights on or near the tracks, as if lanterns were being held aloft, said John Brian, a paranormal investigator with the Southeast Idaho Paranormal Organization. The lights have been seen swaying back and forth as they move up and down the tracks. The phantom lights have always appeared minutes before a train makes its final approach. As the train comes near, the lights slowly fade into oblivion, as if they never existed.

"Pocatello has always been known as a railroad town," Brian said. "It was founded because of the railroad, which is a lot different than most other towns in this area. This is an actual railroad settlement."

The phantom lanterns, he said, are believed to be held aloft by the ghost of a former railyard worker, who, not shirking his duty even after more than a century of change, appears at night to make sure the tracks are safe for incoming trains.

Southeast Idaho

IDAHO IS A SHOWCASE OF CONTRASTING SCENERY. THICK FORESTS AND tall mountains adorn the northern part of the state, while the topography in the southern regions is much flatter. But this southern section is not by any means bare, for here the landscape is decorated with lush farmland, steep canyons, and emerald lakes. One of Idaho's more popular lakes, Bear Lake, is in the southeast part of the state and spans the Idaho-Utah border. It is here where we start this section, with an alleged water monster that supposedly inhabits the lake's depths. But read on and you'll also learn about a Bigfoot sighting, the moaning Indian spirits of Fort Hall, creepy goings-on at a hotel, and more.

Monsters in Bear Lake

You've heard of Nessie, the famous cryptid reputed to inhabit a lake in the Scottish Highlands. Tales of the Loch Ness Monster have circulated for decades, but years before that now-famous monster was brought to the world's attention in 1933, pioneer settlers heard about monsters in several Utah lakes. The most famous of these creatures was the Bear Lake Monster. Rumors of a serpent-like creature that is occasionally seen in the cold waters of the resort lake still circulate today.

The lake, nicknamed "the Caribbean of the Rockies" because of its white beaches and turquoise-colored water, has become a popular destination for outdoor enthusiasts who come from near and far to take advantage of the area's many attractions, including boating, camping, fishing, hiking, and off-road riding.

Long before their current popularity, however, the lake and surrounding area were prime hunting grounds for the Indians because of the abundant supply of buffalo and black bear, from whence the lake received its name. And for as long as the Indians have known about the area's bears, there have also been stories about a monster that would rise out of the watery deep, spew water from its mouth, and carry away members of the tribes as they bathed near the shores.

Stories of the monster were told to the pioneers when they began to settle the valley in the 1860s, and became popular after Joseph C. Rich wrote an article for the *Deseret News* of Salt Lake City. The article, "Monsters in Bear Lake," appeared in the paper's July 31, 1868, edition. Rich told about the Indian legend and then shared new tales about the water monster. It wasn't long after the article was published that the pioneers began recounting their own encounters with what became known as the Bear Lake Monster. Before long, it was common knowledge that a strange, prehistoric creature lived in the lake. According to the book *Folklore in the Bear Lake Valley*, a man named C. M. Johnson claimed he saw the head and long neck of a creature rise from the water's surface. Even Brigham Young seemed to have believed the stories, for he supposedly offered rope to a hunting expedition to snare the monster.

Stories about sea creatures that roam the expansive and often unexplored ocean depths are one thing, but how did a freshwater monster arrive in an inland lake? One assumption was that the creature, whatever it might be, was a prehistoric entity left over from Lake Bonneville, which existed thousands of years ago and covered one-third of Utah and parts of neighboring states. But according to geologists, Bear Lake is not a remnant of that ancient lake, but instead was created separately about twenty-eight thousand years ago.

However the monster arrived, it apparently wasn't alone. In 1871, the *Salt Lake City Herald* reported that a man had captured a young member of the monster family near Fish Haven: "This latter-day wonder is said to be about twenty feet in length, with a mouth sufficiently large to swallow a man without any difficulty, and is propelled through the water by the action of its tail and legs."

Interestingly, twenty years after Rich's article was published, he confessed that he had made up the tales after he heard the Indian stories, hoping to attract attention to the area. Rich's confession didn't stop the stories of the monster from continuing to circulate, however, and more eyewitnesses reported seeing the strange water creature. Accounts have varied: the monster has been described as resembling a walrus, large carp, dragon, crocodile or duck-billed creature, being anywhere from twenty feet to ninety feet long, and being able to swim up to sixty miles per hour.

What do you believe? It's likely that, as with the Loch Ness Monster, most visitors to the lake will not see the Bear Lake Monster. But remember, not seeing it isn't proof that such a monster doesn't truly exist.

Bigfoot in Franklin County

The Bigfoot legend is alive and well in southeast Idaho. High-school students working on a class project reported catching glimpses of the famous creature in late May 2012 while in forestland near Mink Creek in Franklin County.

While the students worked on their project, using a video camera for part of it, they unexpectedly caught footage of a "dark, mysterious creature . . . for a few seconds . . . before it retreated into the treeline," according to an ABC News blog post.

"It just didn't look human-like," the student who recorded the video and who wished to remain anonymous told the local ABC affiliate. "I don't know what that is, it's not a bear, it's not a moose or anything. It was big and bulky and black."

The students, after seeing the creature, climbed the hill to where they saw the "potential Sasquatch" and discovered large footprints in the dirt, which the students also photographed.

The student who was acting as voice for the group told the news station: "I'm not going to say yes it was a Bigfoot or no it wasn't, because I don't know, and nobody knows."

The news apparently caught a lot of online attention, because a month later, on June 29, blog comments about the article numbered more than seven thousand.

Indian Spirits of Fort Hall and Bear River

No one knows for sure, but it's been estimated that more than one hundred thousand people traveled America's primary overland route, the Oregon Trail, between 1841 and 1869. The 2,100-mile-plus route started in Missouri and stretched to the Pacific Northwest. Emigrants fleeing their old lives in the Midwest embarked on the trail in search of new lives in the West. Most went to Oregon, but some parties broke off from the main trail to head to other destinations, such as Utah or California.

One popular stopping point along the way was Fort Hall, located in modern-day Bannock County in southeast Idaho. It was established in 1864 by the Fort Bridger Treaty between the United States and Shoshone and Bannock tribes in the wake of the 1863 Bear River Massacre. In that bloody conflict, more than four hundred Indians were killed by Army soldiers. It was a sad day in the history of the U.S. and Idaho, and the culmination of a long, continuing struggle between Indians and the white man. In the 1850s, Chief Pocatello commanded attacks on emigrant parties, in part because they were encroaching on his tribe's hunting grounds. The violence between the two sides continued for years, and in 1863 Col. Patrick Edward Connor led his troops from Fort Douglas, Utah, to the area to "chastise" the Shoshone. Pocatello, however, was warned of Connor's plans and led his people out of harm's way, resulting in an attack on another band. Pocatello subsequently sued for peace and agreed to relocate his people to a newly established reservation along the Snake River.

Four bands of Shoshone and the Bannock band of the Paiute relocated to the reservation, then consisting of 1.8 million acres of land. The U.S. government agreed to supply the Shoshone-Bannock annually with goods and annuities worth $5,000.

From 1868 to 1932, the reservation territory was reduced by two-thirds due to encroachment of non-native settlers and governmental land seizures. In 1934 Congress passed the Indian Reorganization Act, created in part to encourage tribes to reestablish self-government, and to keep their land bases. In 1936 the Fort Hall tribes reorganized, wrote a constitution, and established their own elected government.

Before it became a reservation, Fort Hall was a fur-trading station established by Captain Nathaniel Wyeth in 1834. His business was short lived, however, at least under his ownership. He sold it a year later before returning to the east.

The fort today allegedly is haunted by a woman who appears dressed in white, but with no face. Who she is and what her lack of a face means, we can only guess. The phantom cries of small children and babies also have been reported near the river bottoms.

As for the massacre site farther south near Preston, it is a tranquil place where visitors come to read the markers and learn about the area's history, both tragic and otherwise. While here, however, you can't help but imagine the ruthless crime that was committed here, the bloodshed and battles. Some visitors say they've sensed the spirits of the murder victims, and some have even heard their weeping. Some with sensitive ears, for instance, claim to have heard crying that very much sounds like young children—even when no babies were in the area. It also is rumored that in winter, the season when the massacre took place, phantom footprints suddenly appear in freshly fallen snow, trailing off into the distance before disappearing entirely.

Ghosts of Malad City

Every town has its ghost stories and legends, every city its haunted house or cemetery. Malad City, located in Oneida County near the Idaho-Utah border in southeast Idaho, is no exception. It is a place where the spirits of the dead walk freely and without animosity. At least, that's what some stories say about the place.

The spirits apparently have been here a long time. Malad City, named after the nearby Malad River, was established in 1864 and is today hailed as one of Idaho's oldest communities. But even before it was established as a town, it was visited by fur trappers and explorers. Could some of the ghosts that roam here be those of some of the trappers—Donald Mackenzie, for instance?

Mackenzie was a Scottish-Canadian trapper who led a party through the area sometime between 1818 and 1821. It didn't turn out to be a very pleasant experience. Several of his men became ill while camping in the area. They determined the cause of their illness was the river, and so they named it "Malade," a French word meaning "sickly." But Mackenzie's sickly river, it later was determined, was not the culprit after all.

Sometime between 1832 and 1835, mountain man Jim Bridger led another group to the area. His men also became ill, but not from the river itself—from the beaver that inhabit it. Beaver, the world's largest rodent, would digest poisonous roots from a certain tree in the area. The roots apparently had no effect on the animals, but they wreaked havoc on Bridger's men after they ate the beaver.

Others who came through the area include John C. Fremont (1843) and Brigham Young (1855). It was Young, president of the Church of Jesus Christ of Latter-day Saints, who commissioned other Mormons to migrate here and build up the town site. Led by Ezra Barnard, fifteen families traveled from Salt Lake City to Malad Valley to establish a faith-based agricultural community that they named Fort Stuart. The following year, in 1857, Fort Stuart was renamed Malad City.

The city, which at one time was home to as many as nearly three thousand people, today has a population of just 2,095, according to 2010 census estimates. It also is home to the country's oldest department store.

The Malad River may not actually cause illness, but its area—including Malad City—seems to get more than its share of bad luck. A magnitude 6.1 earthquake struck Pocatello Valley on March 27, 1975. The epicenter was just fifteen miles from Malad City, which was hardest hit by the trembler. Nearly two-thirds of its homes and businesses were damaged. A corporate jet carrying eight people from Salt Lake City to Pocatello, Idaho, including four Coca-Cola executives, crashed in the city's vicinity on January 15, 1996, killing all on board and making national news headlines. The cause of the accident was ice on the wings, according to the National

Transportation Safety Board. When an influenza outbreak occurred in the area in December 2003, Malad City was reported as the hardest hit. So many people became ill that the city literally shut down. Schools, churches, and holiday activities were canceled.

Does Malad City have a curse upon it? Probably not, but the bad luck that's been plaguing the area since Mackenzie's day makes one wonder if there's something supernatural at work.

Enders Hotel

In the 1980s, Orson Scott Card wrote a story that since its first full publication in 1985 (though portions of it were published in 1977 in the magazine *Analog*) has become a classic of science-fiction literature. The novel *Ender's Game* is about a young boy who is a military genius; he's being trained—through "games"—to fight aliens that already have attacked Earth twice.

Ender is a name you probably don't hear too often. So far, I've heard it used only twice: in the title of Card's classic book and in the name of a haunted hotel in Soda Springs, located in Idaho's Caribou County. The hotel has nothing to do aliens or games, but it does have something of the supernatural.

Soda Springs is perhaps another interesting name, bringing to mind a spring bubbling with soda. Take your pick—orange, strawberry, or cream soda. Well, not exactly. There's no flavored drinks here, unless you purchase them from a grocery store, restaurant, or vending machine. But carbonated water, sure; there's plenty of that.

Soda Springs is named for the thousands of natural carbonated springs located in and around the city. The springs were well known to the Native Americans and a popular landmark for the emigrants who traveled the Oregon Trail. The city today has a population of a little more than three thousand people, and is the location of a man-made, carbon dioxide–generated coldwater geyser.

As for the famed hotel, Enders Hotel is a three-story building that, according to local rumor, is visited by at least one angry spirit. In some instances, the spirit has threatened the hotel's male visitors. Paranormal groups that have investigated the building have walked away with a number of unexplained phenomena, including pictures of strange lights and a skeleton-like face on a wall.

According to IdahoHauntings.com, the male ghost that haunts the building is a clean-shaven middle-aged man who wears a black suit.

Is this the same spirit that visits the hotel's single women?

One of the hotel's female employees reported that a presence would sometimes come into her bedroom at night while she was in bed and lie next to her. She could feel the compression of the mattress whenever this happened. Sometimes visitors have felt ill at ease, as if someone were in the room with them when they were clearly alone.

If you visit Soda Springs, be sure to grab a cool, carbonated drink and book a room in Enders Hotel. And don't forget to ask about its resident ghost. While you're waiting for the spirit to make an appearance, why not try Card's book? I hear it's a good read.

Bibliography

Books and Articles

Balzano, Christopher. *Ghostly Adventures: Chilling True Stories from America's Haunted Hot Spots.* New York: Fall River Press, 2009.

"Bates Motel in Idaho Spook in its Own Right," *Los Angeles Times*, July 8, 2009.

"Floods Threaten Life, Property in Nearby Towns," *The Weekly Press Times*, May 30, 1913.

Friedmann, Kurt. "Warehouse owner hopes to put ghost story to rest." *Idaho State Journal*, October 30, 2000.

Weeks, Andy. *Ghosts of Idaho's Magic Valley: Hauntings and Lore.* Charleston, SC: The History Press, 2012.

———. "The Death of Gobo Fango," *Wild West*, December 2011.

———. *Haunted Utah: Ghosts and Strange Phenomena of the Beehive State.* Mechanicsburg, PA: Stackpole Books, 2012.

———. "Events Throughout May Offer an Interesting Look at Idaho's History," *Times-News*, May 8, 2012.

———. "On the beaten path: The Oregon Trail through the Magic Valley, yesterday and today," in two parts, *Times-News*, August 12 and 19, 2012.

"Mrs. Southard Arraigned: Reaches Idaho from Hawaii to Answer for Murdering Fourth Husband," *New York Times*, June 11, 1921.

"Mrs. Southard Gets Long Prison Term: Idaho Court Sentences Her to From Ten Years to Life for Slaying Husband," *New York Times*, November 7, 1921.

Websites

"About." *The Egyptian Theatre.* http://www.egyptiantheatre.net/about/. Retrieved July 6, 2012.

"Bannock County, Idaho." *Idaho History and Genealogy.* http://www.idaho-genealogy.com/bannock/fort_hall_bannock_county.htm. Retrieved July 1, 2012. (Source for material on site is Saunders, Arthur C. *The History of Bannock County, Idaho*. Pocatello, ID: The Tribune Company, 1915.)

Cipriana, Frank. "Mrs. Bluebeard—She Always Got Her Man: But Her Way of Losing Him Brought on the Law." *RootsWeb*. http://freepages .genealogy.rootsweb.ancestry.com/ ~ smithhouse/smithgen/lydatrue .html. Retrieved July 9, 2012.

"Dark Destinations: Egyptian Theatre, Boise, ID." *The Cabinet*. http:// thecabinet.com/darkdestinations/location.php?sub_id = dark _destinations&letter = e&location_id = egyptian_theatre_boise_id. Retrieved July 6, 2012.

Dayley, Lisa. "Pioneering Oakley Idaho: Museum to showcase new addition during Pioneer Days." *Weekly News Journal*, July 21, 2011. http://www .minicassia.com/news/article_d732ae32-b3d4-11e0-a0a3-001a4bcf6878 .html. Retrieved August 13, 2012.

Dell'Amore, Christine. "New Life-forms Found at Bottom of Dead Sea: Middle Eastern salt lake a 'fantastic hot spot for life,' scientist says." *National Geographic*, September 28, 2011. http://news.nationalgeographic.com/ news/2011/09/110928-new-life-dead-sea-bacteria-underwater-craters -science/. Retrieved July 13, 2012.

Dooley, Bryan. "What does Lake Lowell mean to you?" *Idaho Press-Tribune*, July 3, 2011. http://www.idahopress.com/news/local/what-does-lake -lowell-mean-to-you/article_3b6ec6b4-a544-11e0-9da6-001cc4c002e0 .html. Retrieved August 12, 2012.

"Emmett Middle School." *Idaho Hauntings*. http://idahohauntings.com/ stories/Emmett_Middle_School.htm.

Englert, Stuart. "Silver City: Wallace, Idaho." *American Profile*. http://www .americanprofile.com/articles/silver-city-wallace-idaho/. Retrieved May 20, 2012.

"Fort Boise Military Cemetery." *City of Boise*. http://www.cityofboise.org/ Departments/Parks/Cemeteries/Fort_Boise/page3812.aspx. Retrieved Feb. 18, 2012.

Frey, David. "Hemingway's Ketchum: The writer's legacy in the town that he helped transform." *Sun Valley Magazine*, Fall 2010. http://www .sunvalleymag.com/Sun-Valley-Home-and-Design/Fall-2010/ Hemingway-039s-Ketchum/. Retrieved August 11, 2012.

Goldberg, Harold. "Horror Master John Saul Talks Movies & Books!" *AMC*. http://blogs.amctv.com/movie-blog/2007/08/exclusive-horro.php. Retrieved July 29, 2012.

Gunter, Bob. "Colburn, Idaho History." *Sandpoint.com*. http://www .sandpoint.com/Community/history_colburnidaho.asp. Retrieved July 1, 2012.

"Idaho City History." *Diamond Lil's Steakhouse and Saloon*. diamondlils .net/history.html.

"Information About Ghosts and Hauntings." *True Ghost Stories*. http://www

Bibliography

.true-ghost-stories.com/GhostInfo.html. Retrieved August 7, 2012.

Kameron. "Idaho's Jack the Ripper." *Urban Legends Online.* http://urbanlegendsonline.com/idahos-jack-the-ripper/. Retrieved July 6, 2012.

"New Marine Life Species Discovered in Harsh Antarctic Waters." *Voice of America.* http://www.voanews.com/content/new-marine-life-species-discovered-in-antarctic-thermal-vents—136771683/169707.html. Retrieved July 14, 2012.

Newcomb, Alyssa. "Bigfoot Spotted in Idaho?" *Good Morning America on Yahoo News,* May 31, 2012. http://gma.yahoo.com/blogs/abc-blogs/bigfoot-spotted-idaho-150527313—abc-news-topstories.html. Retrieved May 31, 2012.

"Our History." *Power County Hospital District.* http://www.pchd.net/getpage.php?name=history. Retrieved May 9, 2012.

"Outstanding Trees of Sandpoint, Idaho." *Sandpoint Online.* http://www.sandpointonline.com/catalog/product_info.php?products_id=199. Retrieved July 1, 2012.

Owen, James. "New Species, 'Living Fossils,' Found in Atlantic." *National Geographic,* July 7, 2010. http://news.nationalgeographic.com/news/2010/07/photogalleries/100707-new-species-weird-deep-sea-atlantic-ocean-science-pictures/. Retrieved July 13, 2012.

"Pete's Tavern—Nampa, Idaho." *The Idaho Paranormal Society.* http://idahoparanormal.websitetoolbox.com/post/Petes-Tavern-Nampa-Idaho-971620. Retrieved June 30, 2012.

"Pioneer Boot Hill Cemetery." *HauntedHouses.com.* http://www.hauntedhouses.com/states/id/pioneer_boot_hill_cemetery.htm. Retrieved July 9, 2012.

Phillips, Christina. "The Stanrod Mansion." *Preservation Idaho: The Idaho Historic Preservation Council.* http://www.preservationidaho.org/resources/historical-narratives/standrod-mansion. Retrieved May 21, 2012.

Schlosser, S. E. "Idaho Potatoes: An Idaho Tall Tale." *American Folklore.* http://americanfolklore.net/folklore/2010/08/idaho_potatoes.html. Retrieved July 6, 2010.

"State Report Index for ID." *National UFO Reporting Center.* http://www.nuforc.org/webreports/ndxlID.html. Retrieved July 15, 2012.

"UFO's Caught on news report about fire near Idaho National Laboratory." *Above Top Secret.* http://www.abovetopsecret.com/forum/thread598555/pg3. Retrieved July 6, 2012

"Wallace, Idaho." *Ripley's Ghost Towns.* http://www.ripleysghosttowns.com/wallace.html. Retrieved May 20, 2012.

Acknowledgments

THIS IS MY SECOND WORK WITH STACKPOLE BOOKS AND, AS WITH THE first, several people there deserve my thanks, including my editor Kyle R. Weaver and his assistant Brett Keener. I also appreciate Marc Radle, who did the spooky illustrations for several of the stories.

Many people in Idaho shared personal stories with me about their encounters with the paranormal and unknown. It is those personal stories that give weight and fascination to the topic of ghosts.

Many thanks to Gary Guy, caretaker of Stricker Ranch, one of my favorite places in south-central Idaho; Jennifer Hills, president of the Friends of Stricker; Mike Bower of Realms of the Unknown Investigations of Idaho; John Brian and Eric Aldridge of the Southeast Idaho Paranormal Organization; Heidi Heil, owner of Serenity Funeral Home in Twin Falls; Troy and Heather Mortensen, owners of Albion Campus Retreat; Tony and Elizabeth Woodford, owners of the Get Inn in Gooding; Sarah Taylor, Ruth Pierce, Sue McLimans, and Karen Mattice, all downtown Twin Falls business owners; Jennifer Morin of Paranormal Investigators of Idaho; Ric and Holly Call, owners of Diamond Lil's in Silver City; Dusty Van, owner of the Bates Motel in Coeur d'Alene; Dakota Frandsen, a young but savvy ghost hunter in Twin Falls; and Heather Melton, a believer. It was great talking with you all and hearing your stories. If there's anyone I forgot to mention, it's because of human frailty and not deliberate omission.

My wife, Heidi, has been supportive and encouraging and gave me strength when I felt the pressures of several deadlines at once.

Our son, Brayden, also has gently supported me in this writing project and many others, often sacrificing time with his dad so I could meet deadlines. This book is dedicated to you, son—always my best buddy. I hope you like it. Now that the book is finished, let's play.

Lastly, I appreciate the authors and journalists whose books, articles, and websites helped me in the research and writing of this book. As a fellow journalist, I know how thankless that work can be at times. Thank you for your contributions.

About the Author

ANDY WEEKS IS AN AWARD-WINNING JOURNALIST WHOSE WORK HAS appeared in a variety of newspapers and magazines, including *Fangoria* and *Wild West*. He is the author of two previous books about the paranormal, *Haunted Utah: Ghosts and Strange Phenomena of the Beehive State* and *Ghosts of Idaho's Magic Valley: Hauntings and Lore*.

Other Titles in the
Haunted Series

Haunted Connecticut
by Cheri Revai • 978-0-8117-3296-3
Haunted Delaware
by Patricia A. Martinelli • 978-0-8117-3297-0
Haunted Florida
by Cynthia Thuma and Catherine Lower
978-0-8117-3498-1
Haunted Georgia
by Alan Brown • 978-0-8117-3443-1
Haunted Hudson Valley
by Cheri Farnsworth • 978-0-8117-3621-3
Haunted Illinois
by Troy Taylor • 978-0-8117-3499-8
Haunted Kentucky
by Alan Brown • 978-0-8117-3584-1
Haunted Maryland
by Ed Okonowicz • 978-0-8117-3409-7
Haunted Massachusetts
by Cheri Revai • 978-0-8117-3221-5
Haunted Minnesota
by Charles A. Stansfield Jr. • 978-0-8117-0014-6
Haunted New York
by Cheri Revai • 978-0-8117-3249-9
Haunted New York City
by Cheri Revai • 978-0-8117-3471-4
Haunted North Carolina
by Patty A. Wilson • 978-0-8117-3585-8
Haunted Pennsylvania
by Mark Nesbitt and Patty A. Wilson
978-0-8117-3298-7
Haunted South Carolina
by Alan Brown • 978-0-8117-3635-0
Haunted Tennessee
by Alan Brown • 978-0-8117-3540-7
Haunted Texas
by Alan Brown • 978-0-8117-3500-1
Haunted Utah
by Andy Weeks • 978-0-8117-0052-8
Haunted Virginia
by L. B. Taylor Jr. • 978-0-8117-3541-4
Haunted West Virginia
by Patty A. Wilson • 978-0-8117-3400-4
Haunted Wisconsin
by Linda S. Godfrey • 978-0-8117-3636-7

WWW.STACKPOLEBOOKS.COM • 1-800-732-3669